SEQUENCE
(con)SEQUENCE

ESSAYS BY

Julia Ballerini
William S. Wilson
Lori Zippay

PHOTOGRAPHS BY

Dennis Adams
Mac Adams
Vikky Alexander
John Baldessari
Gretchen Bender
Jean-Charles Blanc
Dorit Cypis
Nancy Goldring
William Larson
John Maggiotto
Lorie Novak
Robert Rauschenberg
Hope Sandrow
John Schlesinger
Klaus Schnitzer/
Robert Sennhauser
Eve Sonneman
Silvia Taccani
Brian Wood

SEQUENCE (con)SEQUENCE

(sub) VERSIONS OF PHOTOGRAPHY IN THE 80s

EDITED BY
Julia Ballerini

APERTURE
in association with the
Edith C. Blum Art Institute, Bard College

Sequence (con)Sequence accompanies
an exhibition of the same name organized by
and opening at the Edith C. Blum Art Institute,
Bard College, February 10–April 15, 1989.

This publication is made possible,
in part, by grants from the
National Endowment for the Arts,
the Edith C. Blum Foundation,
and the Stanley Landsman Fund
to the Edith C. Blum Art Institute.

 Composition by EyeType.
Printed and bound in the United States of America.

Library of Congress Catalog Number: 88-082880
ISBN 0-89381-358-3

CONTENTS

ACKNOWLEDGMENTS

The nineteen photographers presented in this publication, and in the exhibition that provided its occasion, are representatives of three distinct generations. Some have played distinguished roles in the art world for over thirty years, some are newcomers. They were born in such diverse locations as California, Minnesota, and New York, Wales, Canada, France, and Israel. Their work is equally varied. Some pieces must be measured in inches, others in yards. They may be wall hung or standing, brilliantly colored or monochrome, decorative or severe.

Despite the fact that these works represent a great range of photographic possibilities, they have been selected because they all involve the concept of referential multiplicity as it applies to temporal, thematic, and aesthetic formulations. "Sequence" and its "Con-sequence" are the topic that has been explored in the pages of this book.

It has been a great privilege to work with the talented cast of participants who made this project possible. The individual photographers have each provided provocative material that invites critical examination. Dr. Julia Ballerini, the exhibition curator, by grouping these particular artists together, has instigated speculation about the new parameters of contemporary photography (as opposed to contemporary photographers).

This challenge has been accepted and expanded by Dr. William S. Wilson and Lori Zippay, who have extrapolated these concepts and applied them to the fields of literature and video, respectively. The result of this joint effort, encompassing three fields of cultural expression, is a coherent thesis about the nature of artistic expression in the 1980s.

These talents were molded into a book under the astute guidance of Steve Dietz, editor at Aperture Foundation. But effort alone does not suffice. It is the generous grant by the National Endowment for the Arts that provided, in part, the financial support for this project.

The members of the administration of Bard College and the members of the Board of Overseers of the Edith C. Blum Art Institute join me in taking this opportunity to express appreciation to John Pruitt and Tom Wolf of the Bard College faculty for their assistance and to the participants for both their excellent work and the spirit in which that work was carried out.

Brief biographies of the artists and authors are included at the end of the book, evidence that they are exceptional individuals who have all made significant contributions to their fields, as they have to this project.

LINDA WEINTRAUB, Director
Edith C. Blum Art Institute, Bard College

PREFACE

Sequence (con)Sequence originated as an exhibition that proposed to exemplify some of the diverse uses of multiple photographs in the 80s. The prefix *con* of *consequence* is understood as an indication of "with" and "together" as well as part of the meaning of "effect" or "result." The verbal/visual (con)-flation of the title, in addition to being a reference to this duplicity, is also a reference to the temporal and spatial collapses and disorientations that allow for shifts from a logic of progression and conclusion—or cause and effect—toward (con)figurations of enlarged and often oppositional simultaneities.

William S. Wilson's essay, "And/Or: One or the Other, or Both," offers a multiplicity of reflections that cast considerable light onto contemporary photographic practice. With references to linguistics, mathematics, music, architecture, as well as painting and sculpture, "And/or" reflects on uncertainty as a condition (not an incapacity) of postmodern thought, on contradiction as metamorphosis, and on the indeterminacies, incompletions, and ambivalences evident in contemporary thinking and practice as the beginnings of new satisfactions.

My essay, alongside this broad (con)text, focuses on photography as a medium, particularly on the different ways each of the selected images—all purely photographic—effect (sub)versions of photography's direct, indexical temporal and spatial relations to its pictured subjects. The associational play of oscillations and simultaneous oppositions this encourages place these works very much in the midst of a contemporary sensibility.

Lori Zippay's essay examines the new electronic languages of both television (the industry) and video (the medium) as playing a pivotal role in generating, as well as articulating, the radical shifts that characterize postmodern modes of signification in contemporary visual art. The routine fracturings of space, time, and classical narrative of commercial television, especially as furthered by the viewer armed with a VCR and remote control, are seen as they are translated by video artists into new visual significations, a translation also highly in evidence in contemporary photography.

I would like to thank all the contributors, verbal and visual, for their generous collaboration on this project. I am also grateful for the support of Aperture, especially for Steve Dietz's patient and astute editorial input, and for Wendy Byrne's design of the book. Linda Weintraub, director of the Edith C. Blum Art Institute of Bard College, deserves special mention for her energy, persistence, and goodwill throughout this project.

JULIA BALLERINI

AND/OR

ONE OR THE OTHER, OR BOTH

William S. Wilson

My theme is everyday life in the postmodern world, when most concepts should be pluralized: everyday lives in postmodern worlds. Not The Truth, but truths. The answer to the great question of agenda, What is to be done? is twofold: pluralize, relativize, and expect answers not to be one answer. Relativity is not as dreadful as it has seemed; according to the principle of charity, actively used in the philosophy of Donald Davidson, most people's beliefs are true most of the time or they would change them. The beliefs *work* for them, and an occasion of interpretation—speaking to someone—requires that one believe that most of what the person says is true.

The word *postmodern* has been tossed into play. I pick it up and make a pass with it over the array of contemporary arrangements, and the disarray of contemporary derangements. The name postmodern does not lend itself to use like older names of eras and modes. The word was invented when language looked like a game, or like several games with resemblances among them, and when the rules for words, or the rules for playing games with words, required that uses of a word be arranged in an array that has a lot of play—to-and-fro movement—within it. These oscillations might not look as serious as some more stable older thought, and the vacillations that accompany undecidability can resemble mere indecisiveness. But undecidability is not an incapacity, it is a condition of mathematical logic. The mind, Harold Brodkey writes in his story "Angel," ". . . does not cease to feel and wobble—wobble means think." Images and ideas, once arranged in rigid dichotomies, are seen to be hinged together. They can still be bilaterally symmetrical, but they cannot be rigidly determined. They may and do wobble, so that to-and-fro becomes a motion of thinking, even a method of thought, with overlaps among discontinuities.

Word is a word and, thus, illustrates itself. *Postmodern* is a postmodern word and is an illustration of postmodern methods of thinking. *Modernism*, the word, was used as a concept to probe into or to define the essence of an era, as though a medium in art or an era or a concept had an essence. Modernist art sometimes was interpreted as searching for its essence or striving to make its essence fully apparent. Its authenticity would be to do or to be what no other art did or was. The quest for authenticity, in philosophy as in art, is the modernist version of preparing to make a good death.

The quest for authenticity in modernist art seemed to prepare each art for its death, as each seemed to come to the end of its self-critique in behalf of its essence, that is, to come to the end of the implications of the medium. Fortunately, the prophesied end of each art in a self-critique was an inspiration to artists. The modernist inquiry into the essence of an art—misguided because there is no essence—actually constructed the object of its own inquiry. Formalism/modernism, at least in theory, invented gaps or intervals among the arts, which then led to false questions either about a hierarchy of the arts or about other arrangements in a significant form. The falsifying questions of women? Modernism put women aside to be put up for later, when their essence should have been decided upon by the men. Feminism in art develops concurrently with postmodernism as a critique of Idealism, and of essentialism, and is fully postmodern. Postmodernisms present playful arrays, few if any attempts to define an essence, and wavering intervals, with women—once essences are no longer the goal of thought—in the midst.

The logic of modernism respects either/or, a duality of oppositions that can lead to expectations that the opposites will be reconciled in a unity of vision or in the unity of the work of art or in some dialectical movement.

But as Milan Kundera writes in *The Art of the Novel*, "This 'either-or' encapsulates an inability to tolerate the essential relativity of things human, an inability to look squarely at the absence of the Supreme Judge. This inability makes the novel's wisdom (the wisdom of uncertainty) hard to accept and understand."

Any classic certainty, along with ideals such as unity and wholeness, suggests an intellectual and emotional health that is reflected in the integrity of a work of art. The wholeness of an aesthetic structure provided people with an example of wholeness and completeness, as though a rounded aesthetic whole would help to make a well-rounded person. The work of art was utopian in that every part was what or where someone wanted it to be, unlike ordinary contingent and imperfect experience so difficult to say "Yes" to. The philosophers who say "Yes!" to ordinary experience tend to treat it as a work of art, a symbolic construct, the world as a poem, but now the world is a postmodern poem, rather much do-it-yourself. Where classicism tends to offer an either/or choice at a particular crossroads, and while some modernism streamlines the crossroads into a cloverleaf, the converging and intersecting paths of postmodernisms suggest the logic of superhighway spaghetti, because the logic of postmodernisms is less often either/or than and/or: one, the other, or both. Again and again postmodern philosophy discovers that exclusive alternatives are not exclusive and that the goal of finding or working toward a totality or unity, a Oneness, is a mistake and an inducement to philosophic violence like the goal of founding the definition of *the* essence of a concept. When we strain thought to define essences, then the law of contradiction is in force, for essence means noncontradiction; a thing cannot be both absent and present; it is either *X* or not-*X*. At least since Whitman—"Do I contradict myself? Very well then, I contradict myself"—and since Nietzsche, contradiction has been questioned because essence and foundation—the grounds of either/or logic—have been questioned. Either/or respects mutually exclusive alternatives; and/or juxtaposes alternatives, often with a pivot, as a pun pivots between two senses of a word or as colors pivot in various pointillisms. The and/or of postmodernisms will not fuel a debate in which points are made to contradict other points. And/or will not concentrate energy and attention on a single central concept that has a stable identity and governs or determines all details and which as an ideal may require elimination of marginal anomalies that do not participate in the ideality. In liberal contrast to essentialism, and/or tolerates exceptions and must allow turns, because they cannot be prevented. And/or distributes attention across points that constitute a field, rather than focusing attention on a concept that crowns a hierarchy. The energy of the field does work, that is, changes or transforms or transfigures anything that enters it into something consistent with itself, without violating the law of contradiction. The law of contradiction is the background for metamorphoses that are transcendental, that is, in which a transfiguring form is imposed instantaneously from outside, probably from a timeless Beyond, from a realm of Ideal Forms and Logical Space. But when the law of contradiction is felt to have less force, when essence is not abstracted from actuality, and when foundation is constructed and strengthened by what is built upon it, then metamorphoses can occur immanently, from within, as *X* fulfills itself by becoming *Y*, instead of destructively contradicting itself. When energy is understood as the ability to overcome resistance, and/or can be seen to permit an increase in the available energy, because the energy is flowing through the conjunction and/or with less resistance than through either/or.

In this way, and/or is part of a flexible politics. As Catharine R. Stimpson commented, neoconservative critics will struggle against postmodernism: "As they belligerently reduce the complexities of postmodernism to the curse words of 'theory' and/or 'deconstruction,' cultural counterrevolutionaries find postmodernism as convenient a scapegoat as their political counterparts do 'liberalism.' "[1]

Critics writing about postmodernism frequently use the conjunction and/or in ways that modernist critics would be unlikely to have done, if only because it sounds legal or commercial. One postmodern predicament is the possibility of endless examples, an unbounded and scintillant field of points and interwoven peculiarities. Ronald Silliman, in " 'Postmodernism': Sign for a Struggle, Struggle for the Sign," provides an example of a use of and/or: "The issue of autonomy is important in the debate over postmodernism. Writing out of a framework that owes more to Adorno than Greenberg, German critic Peter Bürger makes a sharp division between modernists and the avant-garde based on their different attitudes on the integrity, self-sufficiency, and/or object status of the individual work of art."[2] My dilemma is that I am using the quotation as an example, but I have chosen it because it advances my themes; I could continue with examples or with the themes: either/or. To continue with both, examples and/or themes, would be a postmodern solution to the problem of coherent organization of an essay. It might not be classically coherent, but it would be true (an adequate response) to the relations among parts, since postmodernisms keep saying "also." Silliman is trying to define postmodernism so that it is a single phenomenon that does not overlap modernism, a little too much as though it could have an essence, a stable and definable identity. But that would be to extract the concept from its contexts, which is impossible. No text without contexts: " . . . no text is isolated from its intertextual context, a context which differs for the writer and each of his readers, however, much overlapping may occur. If this is true for works of art, to which the quality of totality often has been ascribed, it is even more so for works of scholarship, especially those that enter into an ongoing theoretical dialogue."[3] Since modernism and postmodernisms are overlapping, but discontinuous, and the essence of postmodern is that it has no essence and must seek no essences, to define modernism and postmodernisms as mutually exclusive is an inappropriate vestige of a leftover modernism. This is not to say that the attempts, like Silliman's, to gather postmodernisms into a single thought are not valuable.

The word *postmodern* does not combine with other words the way modernism combines, just as either/or and and/or are different principles of combination. If a thing or a part *is* as it *combines*, then the rules of combination are part of structure and meaning, and the old rules of combination —classical and organic—begin to look like a politics reflecting an Idealism. In looking at postmodernism, we must look at the different or novel rules of combination. The unity of a work of art has been that parts match, that is, the implications of one part combine with the implications of another part to cohere into a unified whole that can be thought of as or felt to be organic. Classical order works often with isomorphisms, as in Nabokov's *Speak Memory*, where the matches the General uses playfully in a game before the Revolution correspond to the matches he seriously begs for on a bridge after the Revolution. The scenes with the matches *match*, the events are joined by a *bridge*, even as someone sells matches in James Joyce's exemplary story about parts that match, "Counterparts." Organic or classical art requires that implications meet or, as in the etymological *pli*, fold into each other. See the New Critical term of value, *complex*, folding together. The issue is how the parts combine together—who wrote the laws of combination? The modernist work of art may prompt the question, How do its apparently unrelated parts match or combine? But that question grants the work a certain "organic" unity and encourages the critic/reader to discover or to invent connections, that is, to discover implications that fold into each other. The presupposing of "the organic unity" also neglects the unmatching or mismatching to be experienced in a work of art, as well as the work to be done in attempting to learn how to respond to a lack of connection, to missed connections, to bad connections. And perhaps the worst: false connections. Among the novelties in postmodernisms, then, are deliberate mismatching, with implications not folding into each other or not coming into focus on a single plane. An early example is described in a letter that Kurt Schwitters, premature postmodernist, wrote to Alfred Barr in 1936:

> I am building an abstract (cubist) sculpture into which people can go. From the directions and movements of the constructed surfaces, there emanate imaginary planes which act as directions and movements in space and which intersect each other in empty space. The suggestive impact of the sculpture is based on the fact that people themselves cross these imaginary planes as they go into the sculpture. It is the dynamic of the impact that is especially important to me.[4]

The dynamic of the impact, not a classical or organic form, is Schwitters's goal: to provide an intense experience, to evoke indeterminate responses. The lack of a single visual plane in Schwitters's work resembles the lack of a single aural, visual, and/or intellectual "plane" onto which parts can be focused in *Europera* by John Cage: "I think what would be difficult, is to make an opera where all things are connected. But, again, it was difficult [to compose *Europeras* 1 & 2] not because all things were connected but because they were not connected. It's simply the nothing in between the elements that allows it to exist."[5]

Postmodernism is a one-word pastiche matching confused and tumultuous and unconnected postmodern experiences. The word does not match, nor refer to, nor correspond with, experience in the way modernism attempts to match word with thing. Modernism, however radical, still focused attention on coincidence and congruence, on reference and on correspondence, toward the self-validating goal of coherence and self-evident beauty. Postmodernisms vary, wobble, sway, and oscillate amid uncertainties, incompletenesses, and bivalences. *And*, and/or *yet*, postmodernisms do not try to refer to experience in verifiable pictorial or propositional representations so much as to respond to experience and to provide something equivalent to which the spectator/auditor responds.

To give a date to the origins of postmodernism would be to propose a theory of a single postmodernism; but since there are postmodernisms, each having not one origin, but several, multiple dates are possible. One of the most illuminating, because it focuses on issues of art, simulation, spectacle, representation, and image, is suggested by Sandra R. Luft, who declares Nietzsche the herald of a postmodernism in which

> art becomes the only response to the realization that a knowledge "adequate" to reality is impossible. Awareness of the radical contingency of the world forces art to accept its own radical creativity: forces it to embrace the artifactuality of the "real," the fictiveness of truth, the finitude of the world that it makes in the face of the abyss. Art has no need of the illusions of an unfinished world and of infinite progress to justify its own unconditioned acts.[6]

Luft associates Nietzsche with the original creative moment of postmodernism: "The rejection of the ontological dichotomy between the real and the artifactual, a dichotomy basic to the philosophic tradition." G. B. Madison, however, argues that Nietzsche belatedly entered this conversation through Heidegger's work and that the "real" beginning of postmodernism is in the work of William James, which he calls "precocious postmodernism." This theory combines well with Frederic Jameson's description of Gertrude Stein, James's student, as a postmodernist *avant la lettre.* Madison sees James's work as without much influence at the time, and turns to Edmund Husserl's self-deconstructions as the efficacious origin. William James and/or Edmund Husserl. Both.

A history of postmodernisms, alternatively, could follow a history of conjunctions, noting Alfred North Whitehead's comment that ". . . the word *together*, and indeed all words expressive of conjunction in general, without definite specification, are very ambiguous. For example, the little word *and* is a nest of ambiguity." As the unusual and inelegant conjunction *and/or* suggests, the problems of postmodernisms are the problems of conjunction and/or disjunction, of together, connection, and combination, of junction with interchange. E. M. Forster's plea for conjunction, "Only connect," stands as a forlorn or empty imperative when everything is connected with everything else but is also unconnected. Seams, sutures, and folds must be examined thoroughly, as one looks more than one way at any interchange, especially an interchange of images.

The word *postmodern* must be pluralized for infinite possible uses in infinite possible contexts. The pluralism, in a pluralist context, with infinite reciprocal modifications of text and context, alters the implications of images. An image that might once have claimed universality must now renounce the claim. The symbol that claimed to reveal a reality, or the icon that might have made a spiritual reality present, both become quotations from a culture, fragments with nostalgic associations. Like earlier artists, postmodernists use religious images—crosses, nuns, angels—but the implications are different because the context is different: the rules of combination have changed and are changing. Today, a religious image, as a part, seems more provisional than providential, changing with the circumstances which change it, as the religious power of an image submerges in an aesthetic power. An important definition of the sensibility appears in Harold Brodkey's "Angel," in the words of a fully postmodern angel:

> It bade me love incomplete meanings and with my whole heart but only for a while. It told me to be fickle. It said—It did not speak but I say *It said*: you see how I lie, how I twist things—It said that only new positions are honest or possible but they ebb into old ones, into ghostliness and confusion.[7]

Although I emphasize the pluralism of postmodernisms, obviously one person can follow only a few lines of development. The need to sacrifice possible directions, to make ruthless choices with no grounds for making the choice, is part of the tragedy of our predicament, a predicament that necessitates the renunciations of essence, foundation, and totality. One might attempt to isolate two or three postmodernisms among others, with increasing difficulties for discourse. The modes have many resemblances, like members of a family, but are of different generations and do not always speak the same languages.

On this subject of loss of certainties, but a possible modest gain in realism about one's powers, I cite a passage from Richard Rorty, to agree with him on a point which tells me that I have been wrong in much of my thinking. Rorty asks, in "The Contingency of Community": ". . . is there a way to break the stand-off between the traditional view . . . which says that it is always sensible to ask 'How do I know' and the view represented by [Donald] Davidson, which says that, when the chips are down, we can only ask: 'Why do you talk that way?' "[8] This alternative, shifting from epistemology to a conversational discourse, probably has been available since Nietzsche questioned the truth of Truth or since Heidegger offered as "the question of truth" about Nietzsche, "Not 'where does he get it from?' but 'what is he saying with it?' " The choice was indicated by Nietzsche when he suggested converting "It was" into "Thus I willed it." My personal history in modernism has elevated as a central question "How do I know?" At one time I would have responded by citing Nietzsche, Henry James, and Albert Einstein, in various ways, to justify a ferocious commitment to the concentrations and liberations of a single perspective, relative to one point of view, but nevertheless answerable to a consensus or to scientific objectivity. Rorty's revisionist question gives me paradigm-shock: "Why do you talk that way?" But this question is an opening onto a tolerant and charitable discourse. It addresses one as though in a friendly conversation that cannot achieve a totality or a dogmatic conclusion. It also brings the philosophic perspective back to the perspectives of discourse, to talk, which is personal, tentative, and incomplete, since whatever one says is still to be talked about. Rorty describes and prescribes a shift that isolates me from much of my thinking; but perhaps much of that thinking was isolated in an individualist epistemology rather than combining with a social inquiry. Still, I have reservations. Heidegger cuts himself off from "Where did he get it from?" and Rorty cuts himself off from "How do you know?" but instead of the either/or of the two questions, I prefer to wobble between the two. How do you know? and/or (or also), Why do you talk that way? Perhaps I do not understand.

When emphasis is shifted from method and evidence and epistemological justifications to conversation and discourse, even earlier art can be looked at for illuminating reinterpretation. Lawrence Gowing, looking at a painting by Rembrandt that has been identified as a depiction of Lucretia stabbing herself, reads it as a representation of Arria, who, when her husband had been condemned to death and could not find the courage to stab himself, ". . . took the dagger from him, stabbed herself, and as she gave it back to him told him '*Paete non dolet*'—it does not hurt."[9]

In an illuminating reconciliation of two disjoined images, Gowing suggests Arria might be consistent with Lucretia, as superimposed and mutually enhancing images: "It may be that some Lucretias and some Arrias retain certain overtones of the other as additional dimensions of self-immolation, and that we should not seek to isolate them from the supplementary accretion that may enrich them." Arria and/or Lucretia. Thus, Gowing, in an exemplary move, opens up a rather unavailable painting by Rembrandt to postmodernist discourse by making it represent a moment in discourse. He describes the woman in the painting as remaining ". . . clearly alive and in serious communication," thereby showing us how to respond to a painting that is not Rembrandt's "portrait" of Arria, but his response to the story of her response. The painting, then, is an adequate response to the idea of both his and her responsibility to their private or internal discourse on "serious communication," now the subject of Gowing's, and of our, critical discourse on serious responses.

Although postmodernisms quote fragments from the old coherent systems of metaphysics and religion, when parts of a system implicated each other in a tightly woven network that was securely anchored, they more actively confront problems of the immanent and finite. The finite turns out to be incomplete, and incompletable or unbounded, and this incompleteness reveals the indeterminability within the apparently available immediacies. Postmodernisms are accompanied by indeterminacies; immediacy apparently is a version of indeterminacy or is indeterminacy as it is available to experience. The abyss of postmodernisms opens within our own texts whenever we quote, for a text is determined by its context, and context is always that which is beyond whatever is quoted and is as indeterminable as text. So I quote, necessarily out of context, a self-exemplifying postmodern text, as plural, cooperating, and interanimating authors here write that context

> . . . emerges only within and by means of the contexts that it creates as it is created by them. So, the context is neither there already nor not there, and that is why postmodernism is not ironic; irony requires an outside, a place to step back from the context, a topos where impartial, objective narrators are not already figured in the ironies that figure them. Except as illusion, no moment of pure freedom enables authors to *de*-scribe as they de-*scribe* or grants texts immunities from communities of readers. Just as there is no place outside the text that does not already implicate the text, there is no text that does not implicate the outside that implicates it implicating it. And so neither texts nor authors break free of the con-texts they can but parody.[10]

The style in which Stephen A. Tyler and George E. Marcus write is familiar in thinking that is not about postmodernism, and doesn't claim to be postmodern, but which has strong family resemblances. Two following examples of sentences share the sensibility: Gillian Rose writes that dialectical history "suspends the history of philosophy within the philosophy of history, and the philosophy of history within the history of philosophy" (*The Dialectic of Nihilism*), and Michael Dummett mentions ". . . a speaker's theory of what his hearer's theory of what the speaker's theory of what the hearer's theory of what the speaker's theory is."[11]

Postmodernism plays with fictions, mistakes, falsities, cover-ups, delusions and/or illusions, representations and/or misrepresentations, and missed connections; it allows for play within itself as it twists and turns among contingencies. Postmodern and/or polytropic. Polytropic and/or polyvalent. Polymodernisms. It can seem incoherent because it is as though the development of alternative ideas that once would have been found in footnotes is now found within the text of overlapping branching paths. That overlapping includes architecture, too (where what is called postmodernism is not always postmodern in the sense that I am developing, merely one among others, of reflecting the logic of and/or; I am describing a sensibility, not a device or trick or mannerism; architects who respond to the contemporary questions most worth asking will be postmodern in the sensibility I am describing).

So in postmodernisms implications do not meet on a single coherent plane, visually, verbally, or intellectually. I mean something as trivial as a design on a T-shirt, with lines shooting off in differing directions toward no single plane, as much as I mean the writings of Donald Barthelme and Thomas Pynchon, and the philosophies of Donald Davidson and Richard Rorty. The novelty for art and philosophy, that is, for arts and philosophies, is that parts with implications that could connect, or once could have connected, into something spherical are laid out so flat that they become (relatively) implicationless, depthless, and unsphered. Flat means implicationless. Some parts, flattened, retain implications, but too inertly to meet implications coming their way from other parts. What I mean by a part here can be simply illustrated by a name. Sophocles' *Oedipus* is a part, a name with implications of knowing and of swollen foot. *Oedipa Maas* in *The Crying of Lot 49* is a part that combines with or brings implications to the other parts. Think of your own name as occurring within a fiction: what would it combine with? That is, what would it imply for characters, plots, and themes?

The feeling of classic works of art, those imagined as "organic," is globuliferous. The "world" of the work of art has been felt to be like a globe, where implications constantly are turning and returning. The organic work of art, with its organic form of mutually modifying and interdependent parts, has been seen as a self-activating independent structure with interdependent and reciprocating implications among the parts. When the implications agree, the art is called self-focusing. Those parts turn toward each other, approximating a sphere, however misshapen, with an interiority that we can feel we are looking into as far as the limits of our sight: our horizon is enlarged to the horizons within the work of art. Or, experiencing a sphere, we enlarge our sphere. The work of art as an organic sphere is self-integrating, and the self that beholds it is to become what it beholds: self-integrated, or well-rounded. Well-rounded implies that implications meet coherently in integrity and wholeness, that everything fits, that character is consistent with itself. Then the self, or the work of art that seems to have an interiority that is like self-consciousness, seems to have livingness, or a "life of its own," an interior sphere shaped by mutual implications. But in the disenchantments, and disillusionments, of the postenlightenment, the sphere or globe can turn out to be empty. The "logical space" of structuralism is a sphere, which poststructuralism flattens and which deconstruction puts a spin on, throwing a curve.

Implications among parts are in a sense subjective and belong to illusion and relation and representation of interrelations, not to physicality . . . even as multiple dots have a single implication. . . . This subjectivity is why implications came under attack in fiction, as in the French *nouveau roman*, and in the antigestalt or anti-illusion of the visual arts, in what was called minimalism. Objective implications were the point of an art that used neutral or relatively implicationless operations. The attack on implications as *mere* implications, as subjective connections of parts that were not physically connected—an unearned and consoling illusion of wholeness—contributed to the destruction of the sphere and claims of organic wholeness, and then helped to destroy any system claiming to explain a total order. And so the critique of subjective implications contributed to the construction of the flattened and fragmented and permanently partial part, which may or may not be a fabric of implications. Postmodernism can use raw juxtapositions of fragments (as in quotations that do not use the force or meaning of the quotation) or of implicationlessly inert parts or of parts the implications of which have been neutralized; perhaps I can speak of dead implications, like dead metaphors. Much postmodernism in the visual arts works with the frustration of implications, especially the uncritical implications of commodities, when some of the motives for their presence or use are concealed. Ideology, in a sense in which an ideological object (commodity) is one that represents imaginary relationships to other people and to objects (I adapt Fredric Jameson using Louis Althusser), encourages vague or imprecise or sentimental perception, as when a factory-made chair is given a signature as if it were work of an authentic craftsperson. Richard Serra's sculpture *Tilted Arc* requires novel, even creative, responses, so offering itself as a corrective to passive or prepackaged responses—the responses that take no responsibility for themselves—of spectators in the legal and/or commercial environment of downtown Manhattan. *Tilted Arc* seeks to turn perception into precise attention and requires that the spectator offer a response. An honest response is an offering, a presentation, sometimes requiring a little sacrifice, a speculative contribution. The opposite of a commercial sight with its false continuities is suggested in Wallace Stevens's "Adult Epigram": "The romance of the precise is not the elision,/ Of the tired romance of imprecision . . ." The task and the challenge in aesthetic perceptions is to avoid comfortable compromises, unearned satisfactions, and shortcut equilibriums, and the gentlemen's agreements of visual etiquette. Postmodernist implications combine different implications—different tendencies—from those of modernism, and they combine with the experience of any audience or spectator in ways different from the implications of modernism. The style in which parts combine is a content that we must learn to respond to.

One of the troublesome subjects in art is politics, which can become apparent when something peculiar is noticed in the combinations of parts of a work of art. If the parts don't combine in a coherent way, then the spectator's attention cannot simply continue in the hermeneutic circle, from part to whole and from whole to part, round and round and back again, reenforcing formalisms of art for the sake of art. When parts are askew or out of alignment, attention may be thrown onto the artist—the psychology and sociology of the artist—and so the parts might not combine coherently, or traditionally, not as a mistake, but for a purpose, in order to throw attention onto the artist. Some formal "mistakes" can be political in the sense of shifting the plane of attention from the work of art to the artist amid contemporary social/political conditions. Apparent mistakes in aesthetic form are political; analysis of aesthetic form when it contains apparent mistakes must include the political, or the psychological. The lack of connections in the work might say, Look at me! and can seem narcissistic, but Look at me! can mean, Look at my commitment, at my system, even in its disarray. That is, the experience of the formally problematic work of art includes the implications that because of the disconnections one must look elsewhere, to a system, for the interconnections, and one must look to the artist for the representation of system, something psychological and/or political. Looking to the artist is not what it used to be, for the artist's self is not a single stable identity but, in various decenterings, is plural, incomplete, relative, and contradictory, something like a collection of aliases to be used along with the biography as an array of alibis. "Bad form" in the arts is a signal to shift planes from the formal to the political or psychological, and whereas that shift can be an error in modernism, it is a resource in postmodernisms.

The tone of postmodern art often seems ironic, in part because irony involves implications that are available to the speaker/author, and to one part of the audience, but not available to some. The questions of irony in postmodernisms are connected with questions of foundation, of essence, and of contradiction. Classic irony requires a foundation in a knowledge of reality. If no reality, then no irony. Irony requires a foundation or ground from which to operate, and the changes in the meaning of foundation and of ground determine more than one aspect of postmodernism: uncertainty, indeterminability, incompleteness, and foundationlessness. See *abyss*.

Since Kurt Gödel advanced his theorem in mathematical logic almost sixty years ago (and another origin of postmodernism), incompleteness and undecidability are more likely in the inventions of mathematical logic than demonstrations of any absolute forms. The foundation cannot be constructed first, although the structure can strengthen itself as it is enlarged, as weak implications gather strength by becoming points in a field of mutually supporting implications. Jean Piaget writes, in *Structuralism*:

> The idea of a form system of abstract structures is thereby transformed into that of the construction of a never completed whole, the limits of formalization constituting the grounds for incompleteness, or, as we put it earlier, incompleteness being a necessary consequence of the fact that there is no "terminal" or "absolute" form because any content is form relative to some inferior content and any form the content of some higher form.[12]

To be part of a structure implies validity, and the larger the structure, the larger the validity, and the greater the reciprocal strengthenings—but not founded on a foundation. Aesthetic structure is a trial of validity in the absence of foundations. The lack of absolute forms, the impossibility of a foundation that would secure permanence and fix values, whether of the Good or of the gold standard, have an effect on irony. The ironist requires a foundation in order to be in a position to annihilate, at least when irony is an annihilation of a phenomenon in behalf of the noumenon. Those who do not understand an ironic statement are left out of the Real and are, in a sense, annihilated. In the absence of absolute foundations, and within the pluralisms of relativities and pragmatisms, and encouraged by the charities of Donald Davidson and others, irony becomes the "blank irony" discussed by Frederic Jameson in "Postmodernism, or The Cultural Logic of Capitalism," an essay I am following with plural gratitudes and my own non sequiturs. "Blank" irony I interpret as the irony that arises from foundationlessness. Foundationlessness supports an irony that dissolves idealist irony. And foundationless irony raises questions of sincerity. There is not and cannot be, as Donald Davidson has pointed out in a quiet but devastating way, a conventional sign for sincerity. Attempts at such signs can be seen in acting and in commercials performed by actors (who do have conventional signs for insincerity, like the wink; supercilious villains are easier to know how to respond to than saints who have no signals for sanctity). In an era of semiotic interpretations, sincerity falls through the net. If one is interested in sincerity, one is in for trouble in postmodernisms, which, acutely aware of semiotics, of signs and codes, often abjure sincerity, and hence will seem un-sincere. This un-sincerity registers as ironic, since irony sometimes entails saying the opposite of what one means. Postmodernism can seem lukewarmly ironic because it skips the usual noises about sincerity; or it can seem facetious, not quite serious, as though playing a game, or as though playing too hypothetically. The presentation or representation—the display—of sincerity in an era of semiotics would require violence, insofar as aesthetic violence is an attempt to *prove* sincerity, and/or authenticity. Most of postmodernism is not so much ironic, even blankly or materially or foundationlessly ironic, as un-sincere. It is too sophisticated to attempt to signal what cannot be signaled. The route beyond postmodern will not be anti-postmodern, it will be non- or antisemiotic. Perhaps there will be something to say about what cannot be signaled: "How difficult, my love, to separate/The silence of what need not be said from the silence/ Of what cannot" (L.S. Asekoff, "Winter Oranges"). Hans Blumenberg ends his *Work on Myth*: "But what if there were still something to say, after all?" Semiotics is the Cubism of meaning, oddly preserved in postmodernisms. But what can be signaled has no necessary reciprocal or mutual implications for love and/or sincerity, which will outlast the Signifier and its will-o'-the-wisp, the Signified.

Because a postmodernist cannot build a foundation before constructing a construction, the image of foundation must be replaced. Perhaps thread (or cord) is a better image, as in the words of Ludwig Wittgenstein: "And the strength of the thread does not reside in the fact that some one fibre runs through its whole length, but in the overlapping of many fibres." A similar point is made by Donald Davidson: "The present thought is rather to expect to find a minimum of information about the correctness of the theory at each single point; it is the potential infinity of points that makes the difference. A strong theory weakly supported, but at enough points, may yield all the information we need about the atoms and molecules—in this case, the words and sentences."[13] With Davidson, we are not likely to go after the essence of anything, but will attempt to render or to convey a field with fluctuations and overlappings. To put the point simply: a promise to analyze THE art of THE novel is a false and destructive promise, implying universals and essences that do not and cannot exist, an Ideal of the novel, and any such statements about the essence of an art are presumptuous and misleading, and necessarily conceal their foundationlessness, instead of working with it.

Rethinking universals and essences has permitted an appreciation of experience and of developments in history as anomalous contingencies, and developments within history have permitted further rethinking of universals and essences. The history of historical materialism, with all seeds of action, all efficacies, within time and contingent causalities, is the history of universals and of essences replaced by history as the production of relations and the relations of production. The universal and ideal and essence is, for the most part, consigned to the dump, as in Wallace Stevens's "The Man on the Dump": "Where was it one first heard of the truth? The the?" Or, adding emphasis, the THE. Harold Brodkey writes in his short story "Largely an Oral History of My Mother," "The comfort and shock of using tremendous abstract terms as truth—when how can they be true? in what way can they be true? permits us to explain a fleshly event without having to toy with the enormous emotions of actuality." George Oppen writes, "Poetry; the experience of the the, the experience of the a within what we thought was the the, they have shown us a billion a's."[14] So white, for example, is pluralized into a family of whites, as Jorie Graham describes apple blossoms : "chalk, lily, milk,/titanium, snow—/ as far as I can say/ these appleblossoms house/ five shades of white . . ." ("My Garden, My Delight").

I am not pointing to a founding father of an absolute idea as I point to Ludwig Wittgenstein ranging over the playing fields of language. He defines "game" without founding an essential meaning: "We see a complicated network of similarities, sometimes similarities of details." "I can think of no better expression to characterize these similarities than 'family resemblance'; for the various resemblances between members of a family: build, features, colour of eyes, gait, temperament, etc. etc. overlap and criss-cross in the same way. —And I shall say: 'games' form a family."[15] A family, whatever else it may be, is plural, with continuities and/or discontinuities, and overlappings, but with no single common denominator. So I shall say, postmodernisms form a family, which I also, for other purposes, call an array, which is like a spectrum with contingencies.

Postmodernisms do not have a single central governing principle, but they tend to combine against some earlier modes of thought, especially against the binary, the dualistic. Two is involved, not as the choice between two exclusive alternatives, either/or, but as the choice of two alternatives: both. The structure of the two cannot be a one-to-one isomorphism, analogy, allegory, or correspondence, in which one object or image might be mapped onto the other point for point. Mapping cannot adequately represent indeterminacies.

One solution to the old dichotomies is the waver, the varying interval. If one, in the earlier modes, defined the essence of something like art, or nature, or business and/or industry, then the definition would establish unvarying intervals among the concepts. Robert Smithson worked with art, nature, and industry by accepting a commission from an incorporated business to make a work of art outdoors, using the waste from the industry to construct an artificial pond; and he expected to reconcile the opposites in a dialectic. My thought is less about any dialectical resolution and reconciliation than about uncertain waverings . . . "The intervals among art, nature, and industry are set in motion." Smithson bought stock in the company that commissioned his art:

> When Smithson as an artist becomes a businessman and owns shares in the corporation which would own Tailings Pond, does he see himself in the company? Is his purchase an aesthetic act, combining art and industry? Or is it a practical act? How would one differentiate the aesthetic judgment from the practical judgment? The lack of differentiation is exciting and frightening, and on one level might indicate a common-sense detour around Kant's differentiation of the aesthetic. The gesture successfully intertwines art, nature, and capitalist industry, and introduces into each concept an abrasive particularity from a possible opposite.[16]

Thought, which uses the opposites that it constructs, invents, or otherwise devises, has long been thinking about how to reconcile its opposites, after it has constructed them, into unity, or Unity, and totality, or Totality, and oneness (Oneness). The strain on thought to unify and to totalize is released when postmodernist philosophy accepts dualities that cannot be reconciled into oneness. Postmodernist structure lays out, side-by-side or in tandem, two thoughts that are not reducible to one, that do not inspire paradoxes and do not suggest reconciliations in a totality. The point is to rest contentedly and tolerantly, not merely with relativities and contingencies, but with a concordant heterogeneity, balancing between coordination and discoordination, and learning to be satisfied with the dualism.

Arthur Danto writes of a dualism:

> Elsewhere I have sought to argue for a materialistic account of representations, to which I can merely allude here. But representations, just because they admit of assessment in terms of truth and falsity, are logically external to the world in which they may in every other respect be located. As agent and knowers, indeed, we are within the world under the concept of causation, and external to it under the concept of truth. Within and without the world at once: that is the philosophical structure of man.[17]

If Danto is right, some of the grief over the human condition, and some descriptions of alienation, are unnecessary, and living with the (wavering) dualism may be philosophic, in the old sense of resignations and/or renunciations. Hence the tone of Willard Quine in *Quiddities*, " . . . the age-old mind-body dualism goes on, then, transmuted and transplanted as a dualism of concepts or language. As such it remains irreducible; but it is out now where we can see where we stand and what we are dealing with."

Thomas Nagel does not reconcile the opposition between the subjective and the objective, to take another pair of terms that have been opposed. He leaves the polarity, but with some wavering or varying in the intervals. Sartre had tried to swallow subjectivity in objectivity: "I shall give the name subjectivity to the objectivity which I have not chosen." Nagel writes:

> The task of accepting the polarity [between subjectivity and objectivity] without allowing either of its terms to swallow the other should be a creative one. It is the aim of eventual unification that I think is misplaced, both in our thoughts about how to live and in our conception of what there is. The coexistence of conflicting points of view, varying in detachment from the contingent self, is not just a practically necessary illusion but an irreducible fact of life.[18]

The point here is the irreducibility of two to one as an irreducible fact of our (philosophic) life: within and without the world at once; subjective, and/or objective. Both. Also.

Within the postmodernism that I am describing, with the logic of and/or, can be found the seeds of new satisfactions, especially if we can learn to conclude with the inconclusive. So A. R. Ammons concludes the poem that could stand as epigraph to every essay on postmodernisms, "Corsons Inlet":[19]

> I see narrow orders, limited tightness, but will
> not run to that easy victory:
> still around the looser, wider forces work:
> I will try
> to fasten into order enlarging grasps of disorder, widening
> scope, but enjoying the freedom that
> Scope eludes my grasp, that there is no finality of vision,
> that I have perceived nothing completely,
> that tomorrow a new walk is a new walk.

1. Catharine R. Stimpson, "Travels with Aunt Chloe," *The Village Voice Literary Supplement* No. 68 (October 1988), p. 17.

2. Ronald Silliman, " 'Postmodernism': Sign for a Struggle, Struggle for the Sign," *Poetics Journal* 7 (September 1987): 25.

3. Martin Jay, *Marxism and Totality* (Berkeley: University of California Press, 1984), p. 15.

4. Paul Elderfield, *Kurt Schwitters* (New York: Thames and Hudson, 1985).

5. John Cage, program *Europa I & II*, Pepsico Summerfare, Purchase, New York, 1988.

6. Sandra R. Luft, "The Legitimacy of Hans Blumenberg's Conception of Originary Activity," *Annals of Scholarship* 5, no. 1 (Fall 1987): 20.

7. Harold Brodkey, "Angel," *Stories in an Almost Classical Vein* (New York: Alfred A. Knopf, 1988).

8. Richard Rorty, "The Contingency of Selfhood," *Contingency, Irony, and Solidarity*, (New York: Cambridge University Press, 1989).

9. Lawrence Gowing, "Rembrandt in Bereavement," *The Times Literary Supplement of London*, July 1, 1988, p. 732.

10. Stephen A. Tyler and George E. Marcus, "Comments," on Marilyn Strathern, "Out of Context: The Persuasive Fictions of Anthropology," *Current Anthropology* 28 (June 1987): 276.

11. Michael Dummett, "A Nice Derangement of Epitaphs: Some Comments on Davidson and Hacking," in *Truth and Interpretation*, ed. Ernest LePore (Oxford, England: Basil Blackwell, 1986), p. 470.

12. Jean Piaget, *Structuralism* (New York: Basic Books, 1971), p. 140.

13. Donald Davidson, "Reality without Reference," *Inquiries into Truth and Interpretation*, (Oxford, England: Oxford University Press, 1985), p. 225.

14. George Oppen, "Meaning Is to Be Here," *Conjunctions* no. 10.

15. Ludwig Wittgenstein, *Philosophical Investigations* (New York: Macmillan, 1968).

16. William S. Wilson, "Robert Smithson: Non-Reconciliations," *Arts Magazine*, May 1978, p. 108.

17. Arthur Danto, "Action, Knowledge, and Representation," in *Action Theory*, ed. M. Brand and D. Walton (Dordrecht, Netherlands: 1976), p. 24.

18. Thomas Nagel, "Subjective and Objective," in *Mortal Questions* (New York: Cambridge University Press, 1985), p. 213.

19. A. R. Ammons, "Corsons Inlet," *Collected Poems, 1951–1971* (New York: W.W. Norton, 1972).

SEQUENCE (con)SEQUENCE

(sub)VERSIONS OF PHOTOGRAPHY IN THE 80s

Julia Ballerini

Fragmentary and discontinuous, many contemporary groupings of photographs appear to allude to (not illustrate, nor narrate) psychic spills and halts and breaks. Remnants of the instability of signification, sequential non sequiturs and apparently haphazard contiguities all appear to approximate experiences of channel switching, magazine flipping, and the general image scuffle of contemporary experience.

But photographs, so much a part of our daily lives, when pulled aside by "Art" from the fraying of their ordinary locations, become highly self-conscious. They refer back to their origins in a different voice; one that is other than approximate. These photographs are not (or, in many cases, are no longer) on television screens, nor in magazines, bureau drawers, family albums, nor on billboards. They have been positioned for longer observations—placed into formats for looking. Their positions in a book and a gallery loosen their ties to their possible utilitarian lives (actual or presumed), and their various configurations within the forms of the diptych, triptych, grid, cross, totem, and array suggest a complexity of other potential attachments, detachments, and reconfigurations.

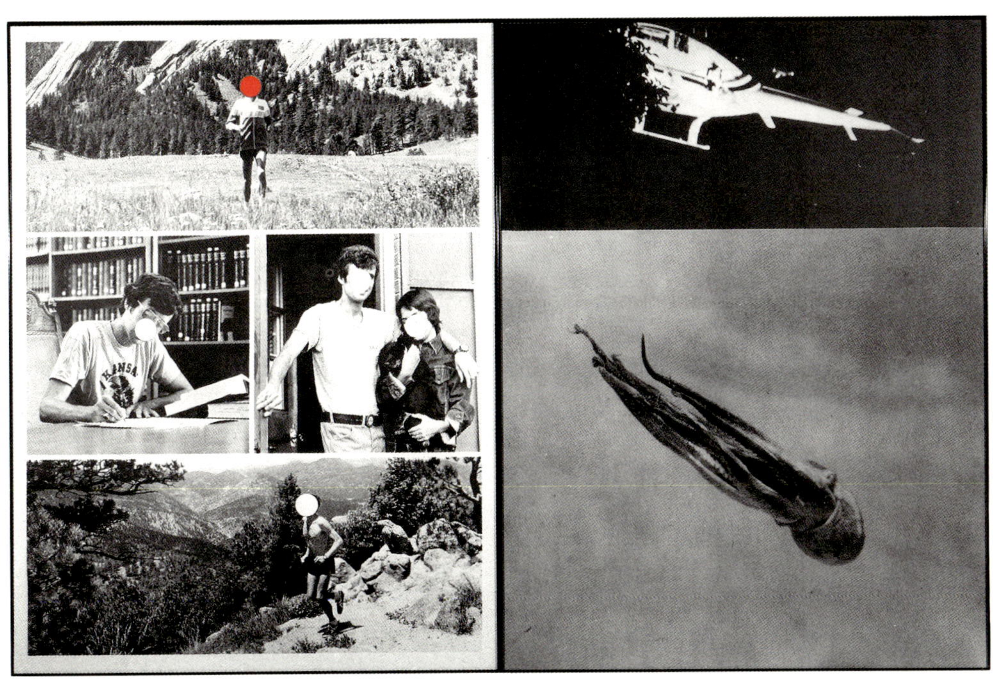

John Baldessari, *A Healthy Life (With Jogger)*, 1987

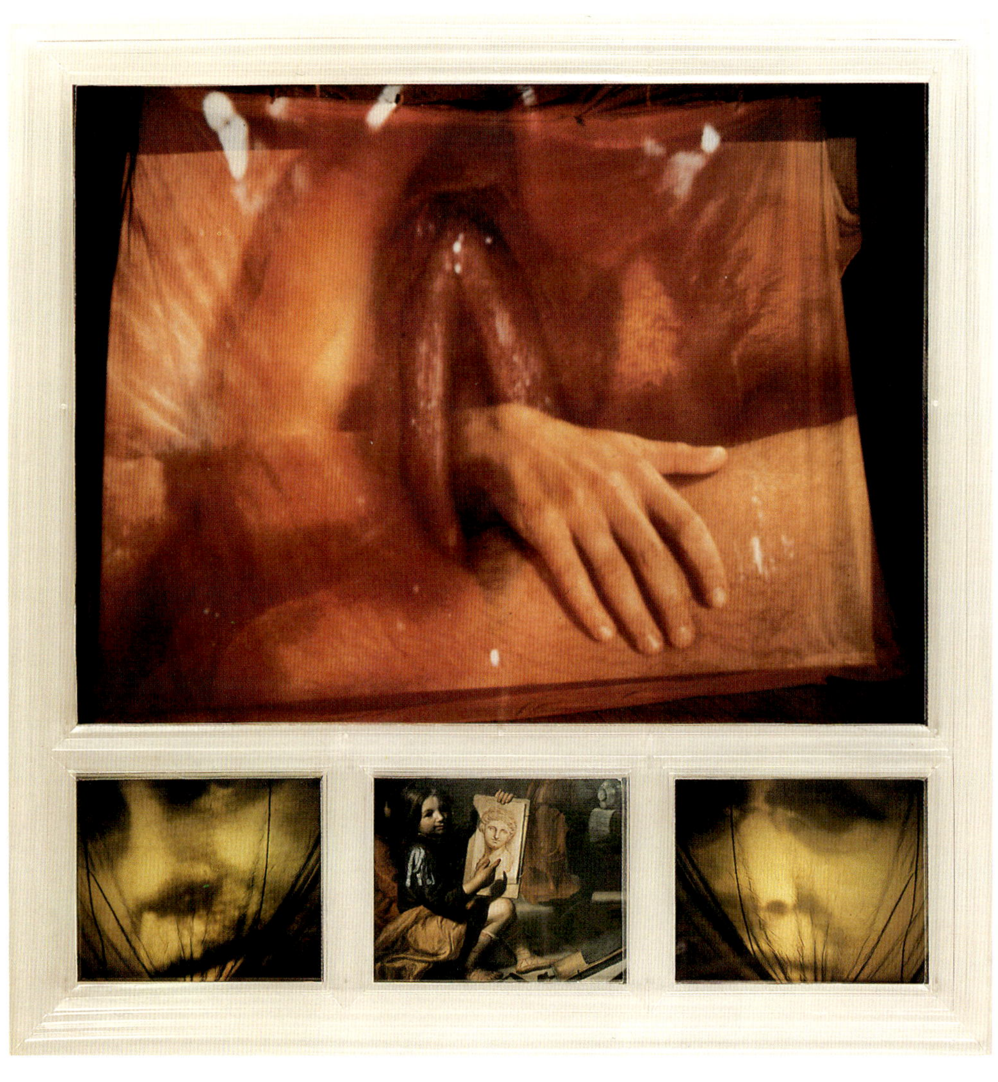

Dorit Cypis, *Love After Death*, 1986

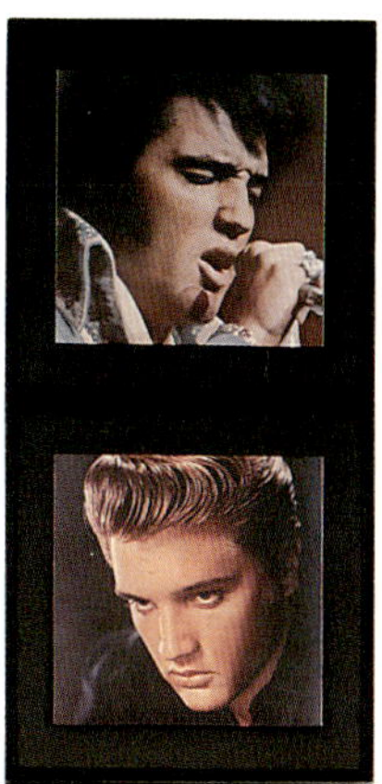

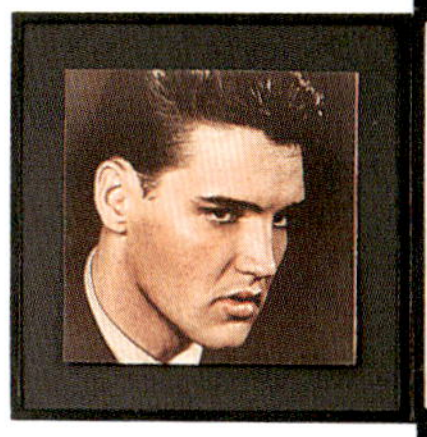

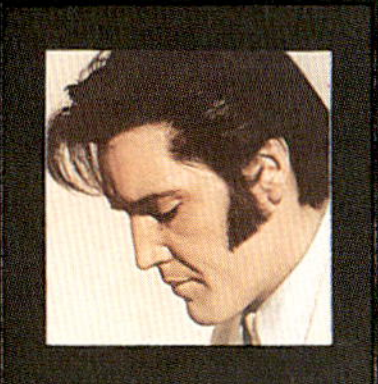

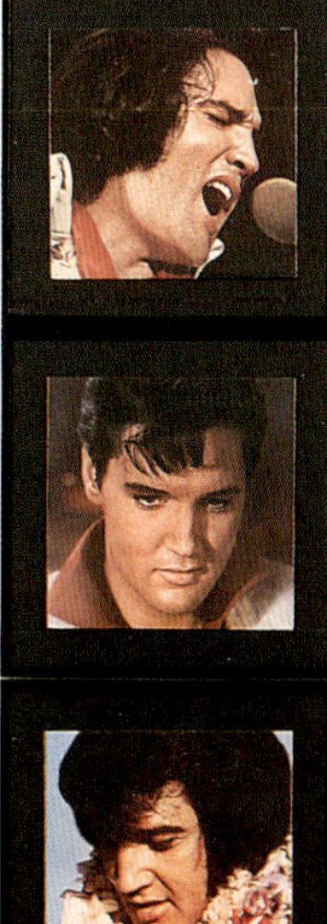

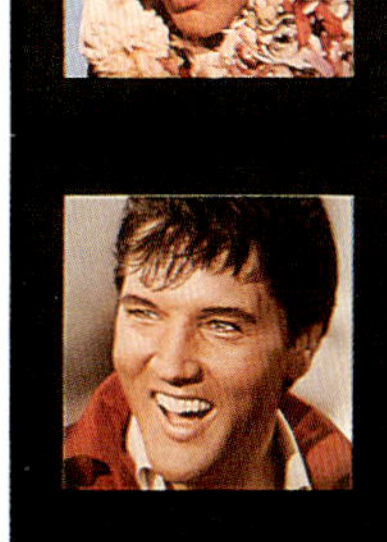

Vikky Alexander, *Grace*, 1984

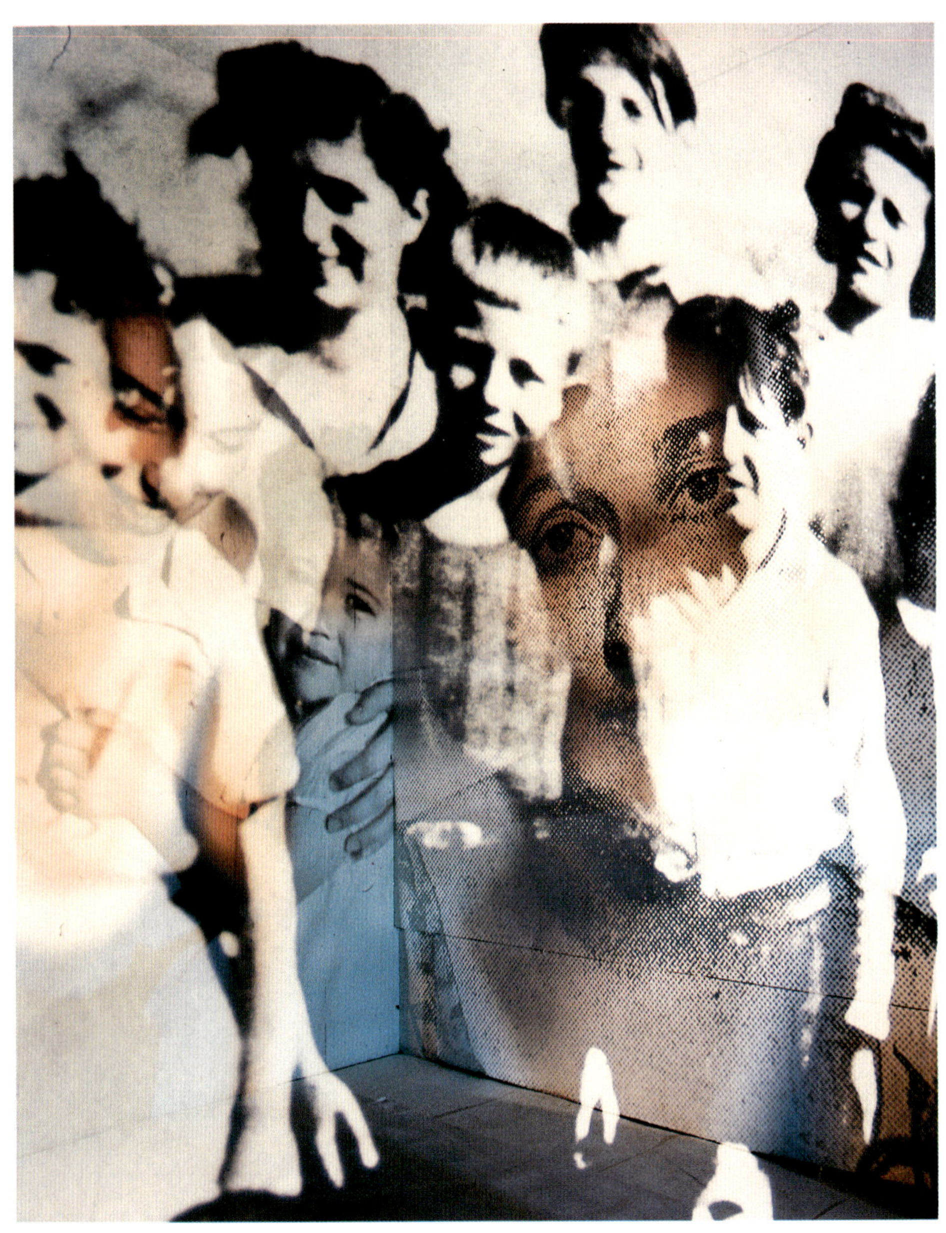

Lorie Novak, *Fragments*, 1987

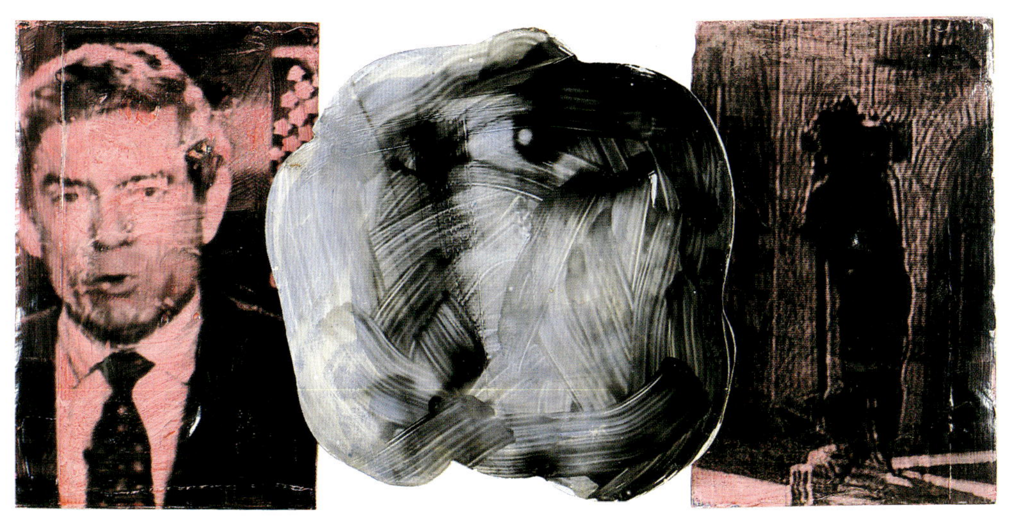

John Maggiotto, Untitled, 1987

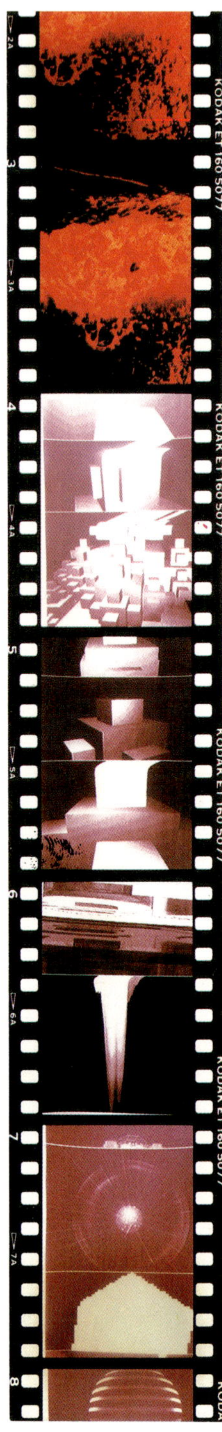

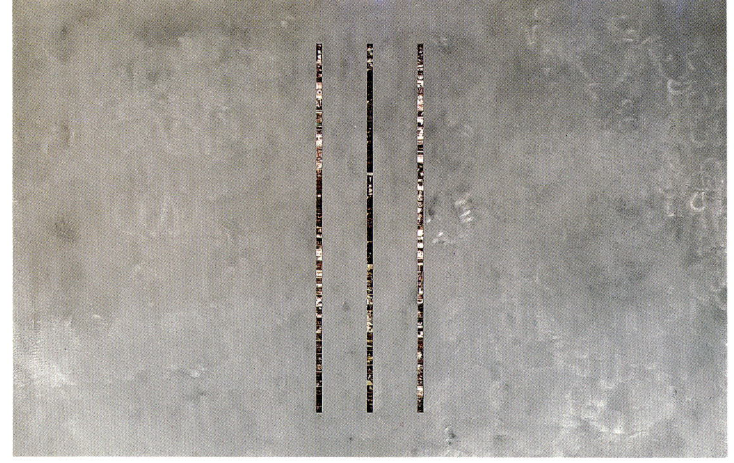

Gretchen Bender, Untitled, from *Total Recall* series, 1986; and detail

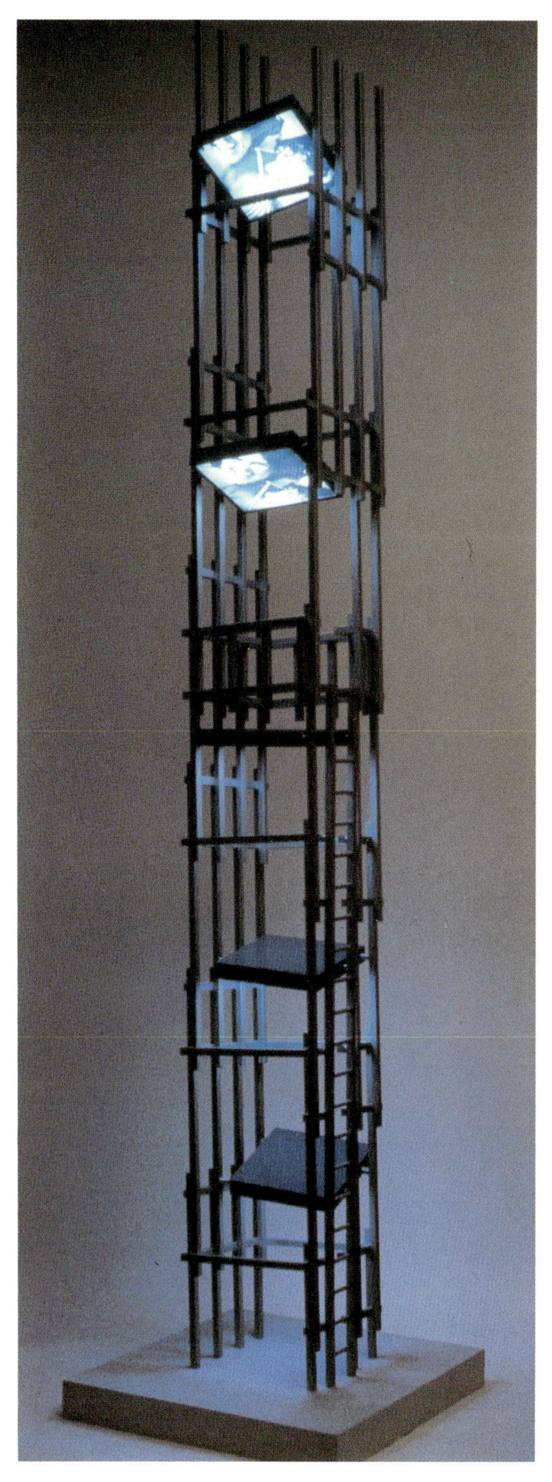

Dennis Adams,
Ba(bb)le: Podium for Dissent
1984, maquette

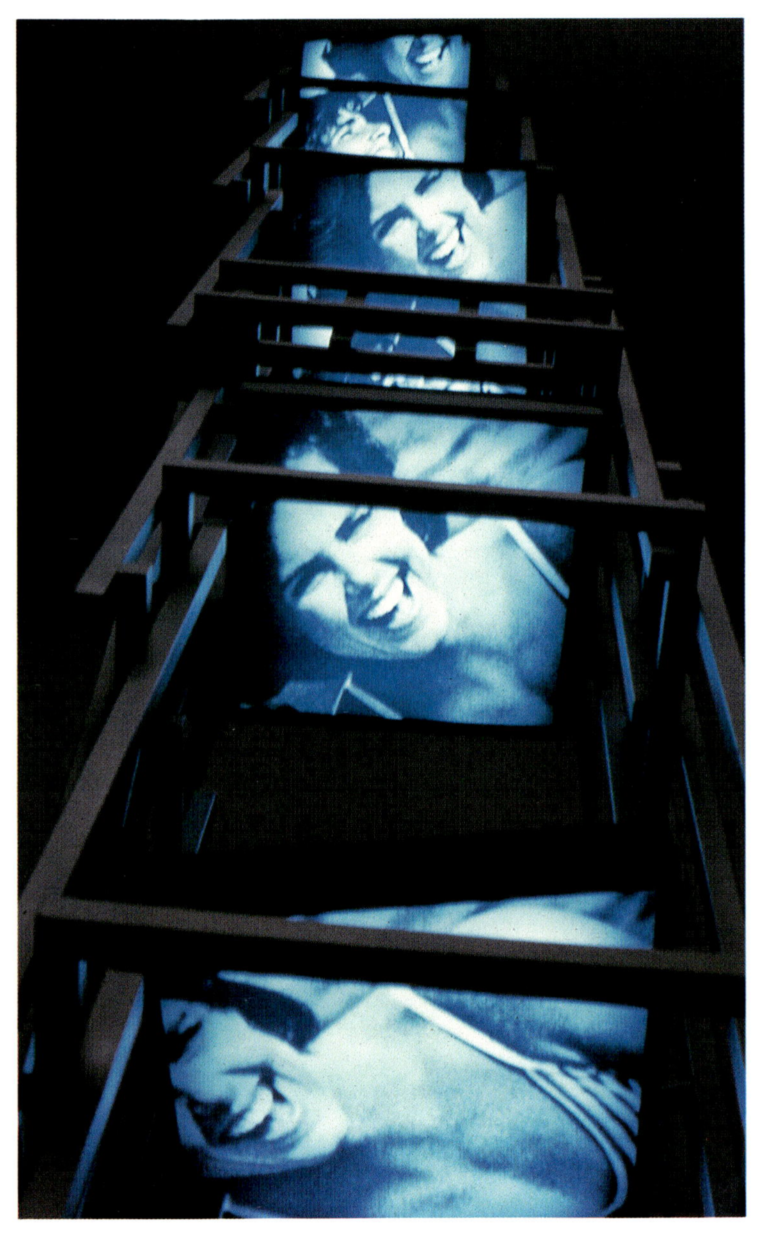

Dennis Adams, *Ba(bb)le: Podium for Dissent*, 1984, maquette, detail

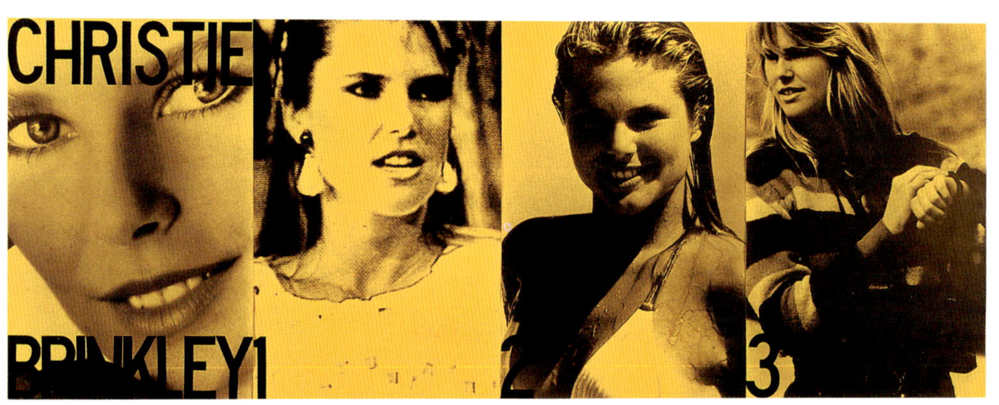

Vikky Alexander, *Obsession*, 1983, detail

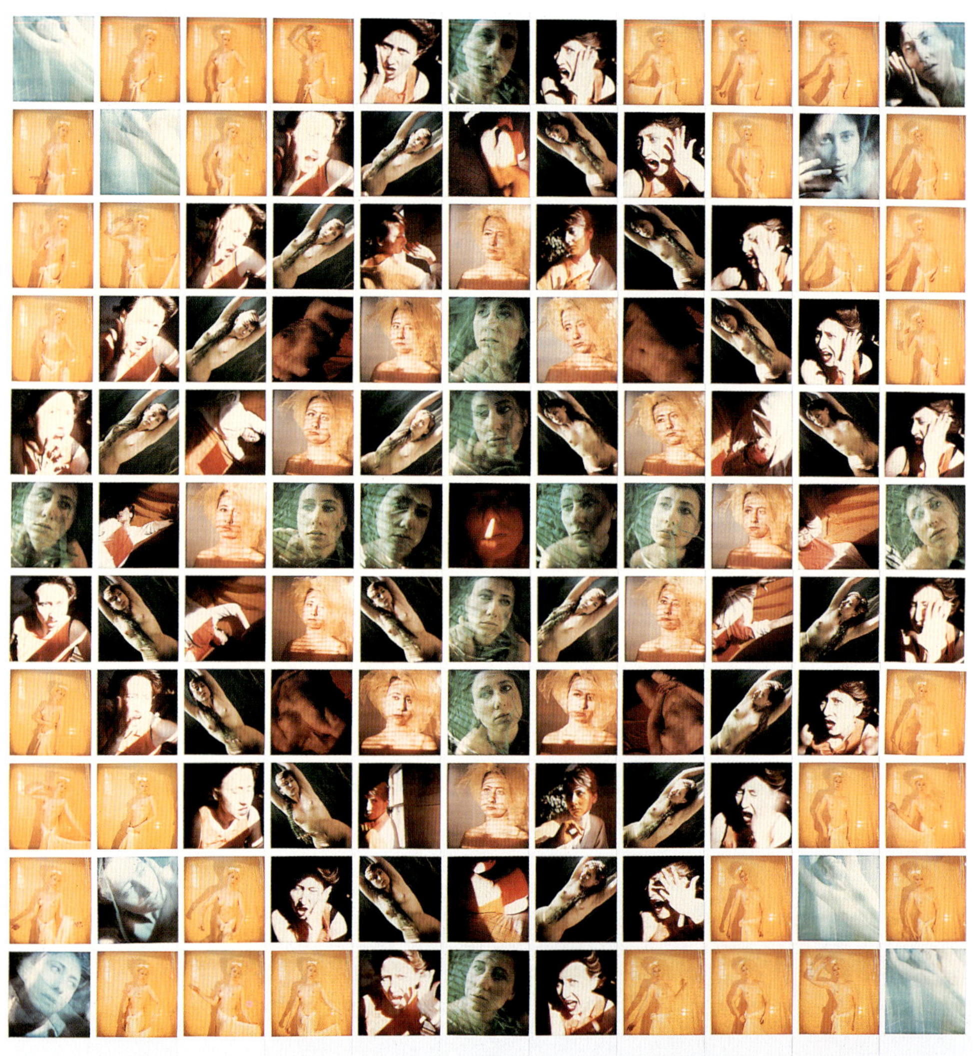

Silvia Taccani, *#91–1986*, 1986

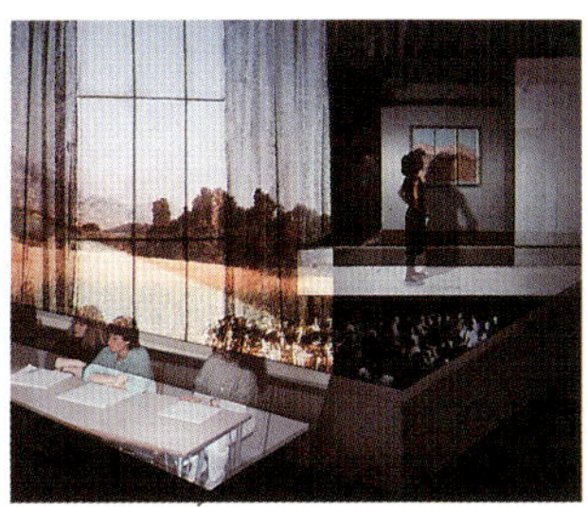
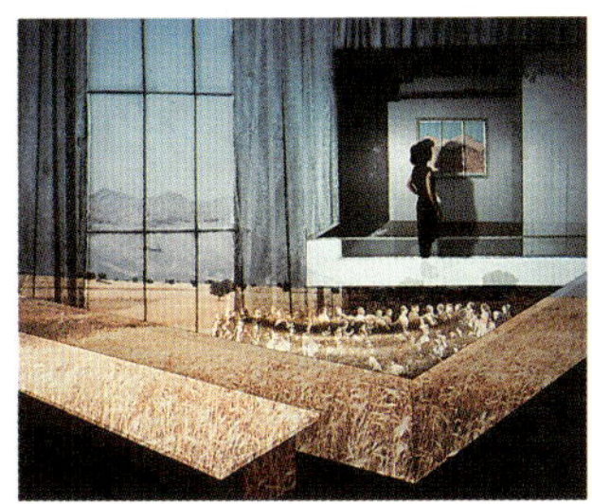
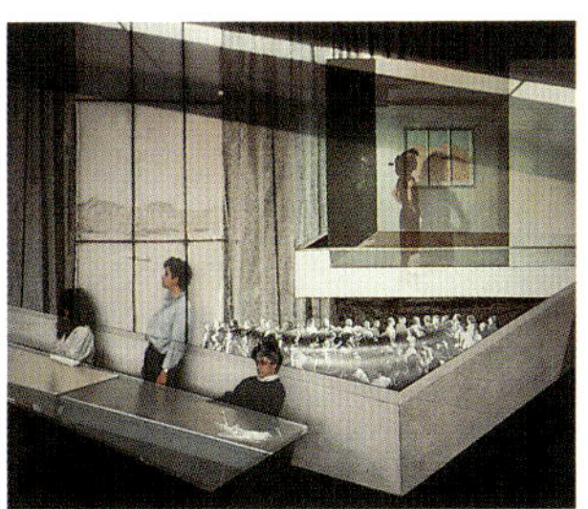
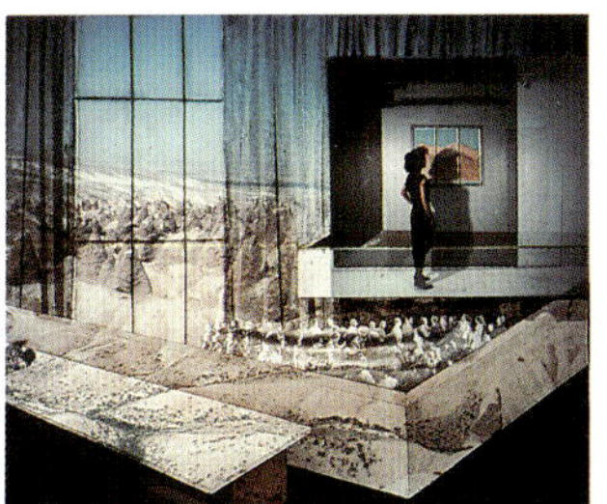
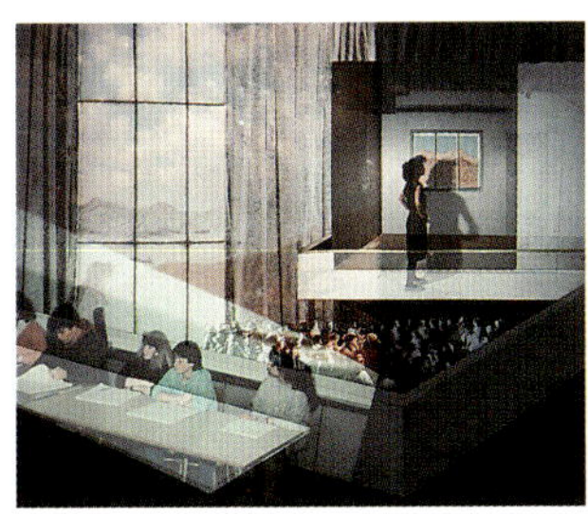
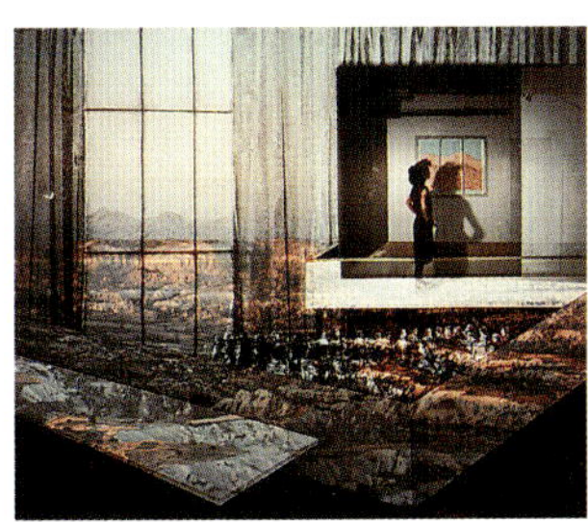

Nancy Goldring, *The Traveler Remembers*, 1987

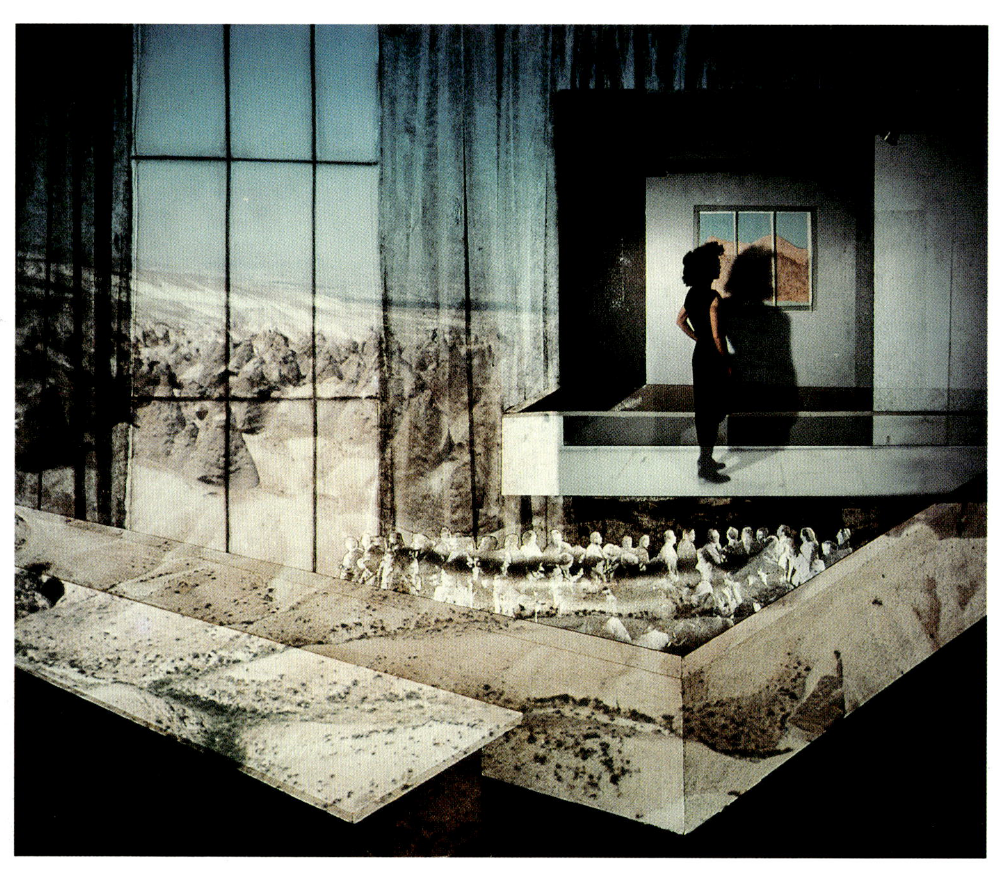

Nancy Goldring, *The Traveler Remembers*, 1987, detail

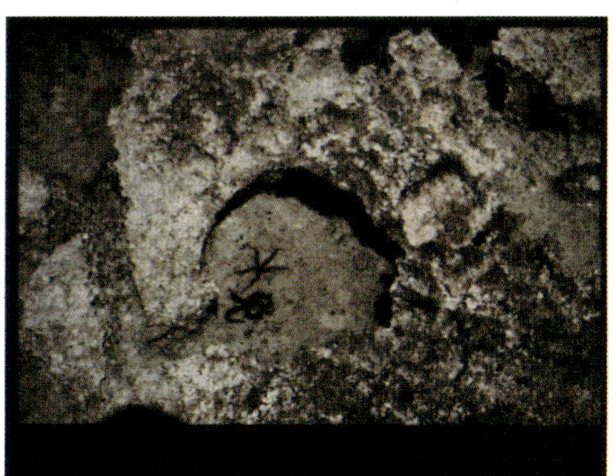
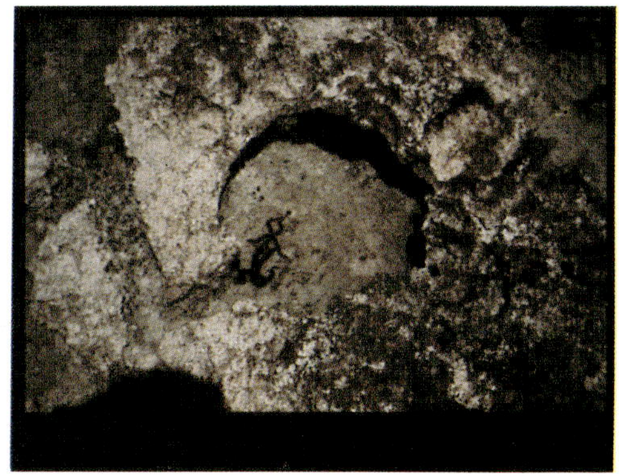

Eve Sonneman, *Starfish, New Mexico*, 1980

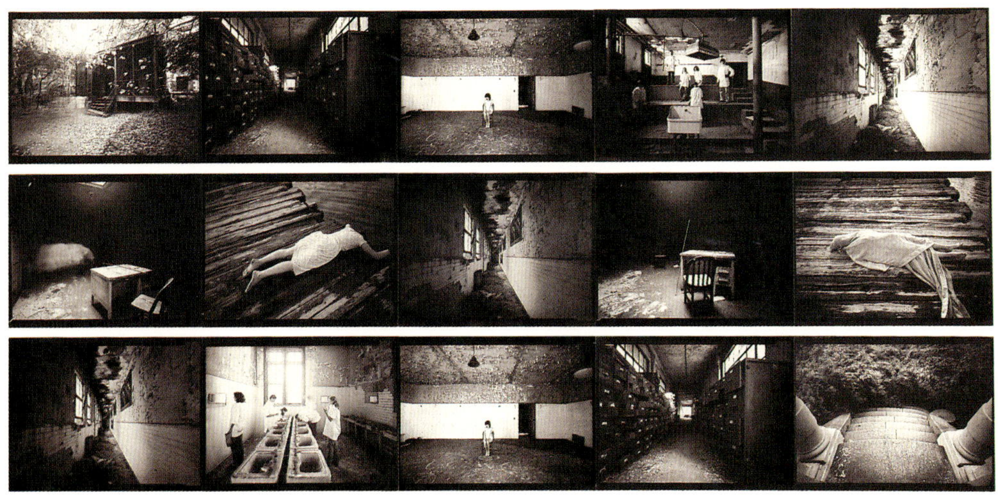

Klaus Schnitzer/Robert Sennhauser, *Timerman's Dream* from *Terrorist* series, 1986

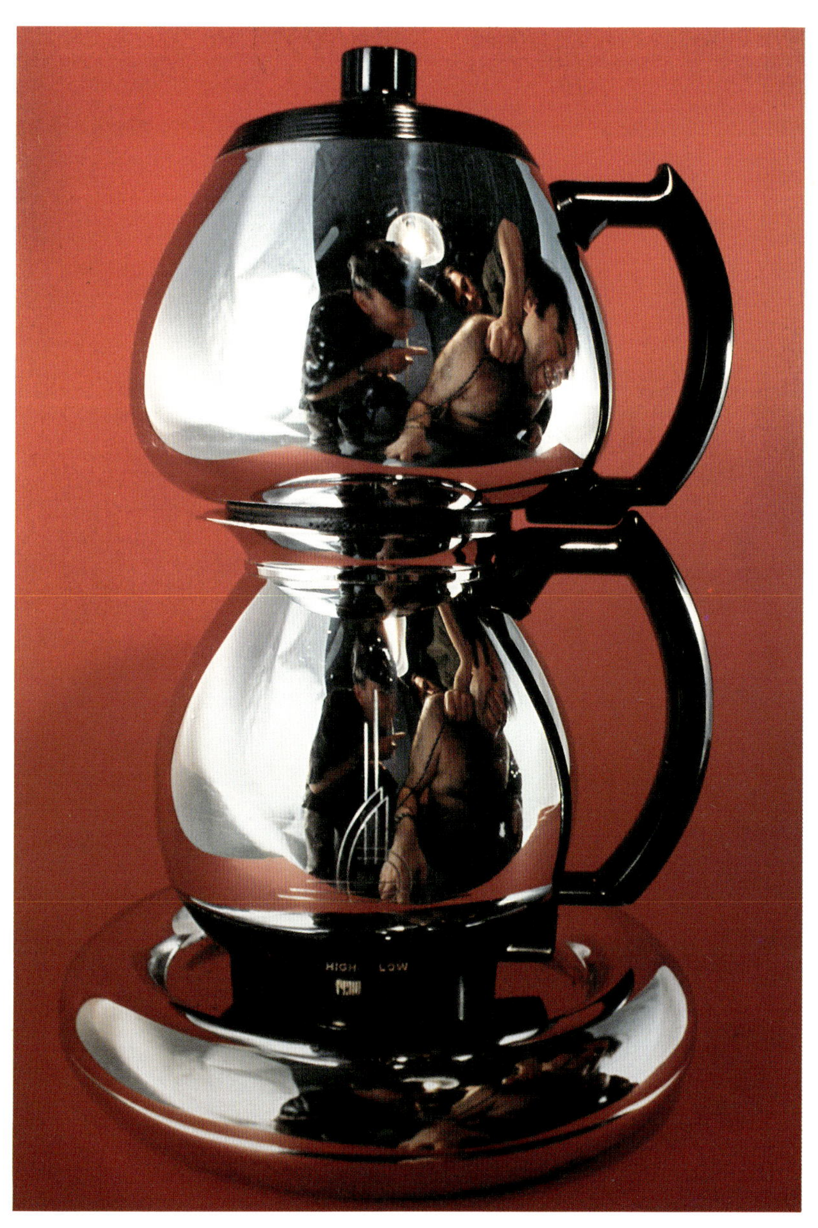

Mac Adams, *Trapped*, 1986

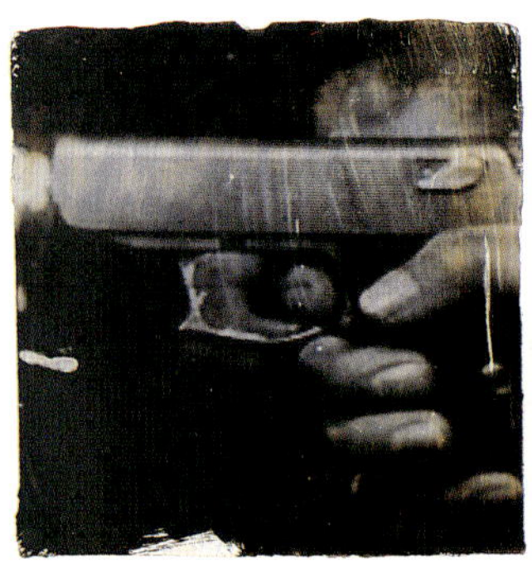  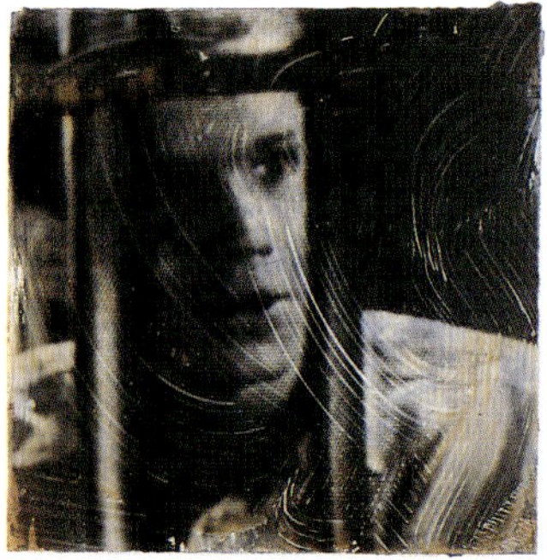

John Maggiotto, Untitled, 1988

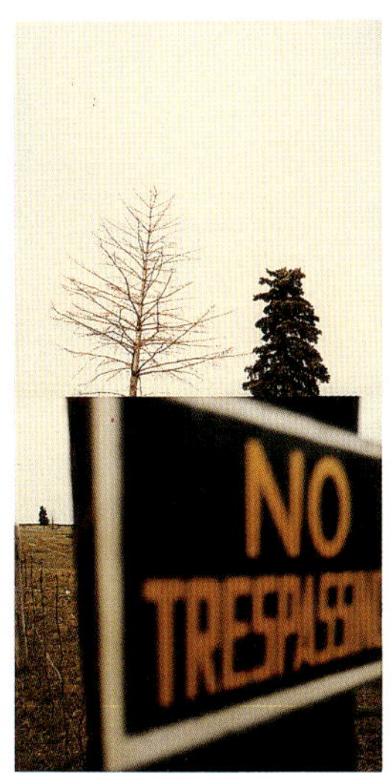

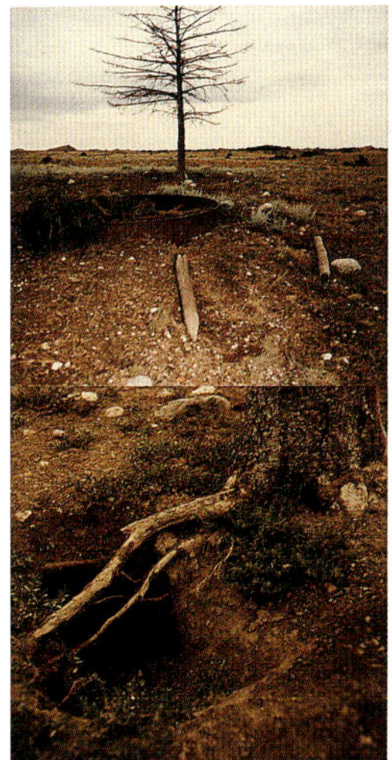

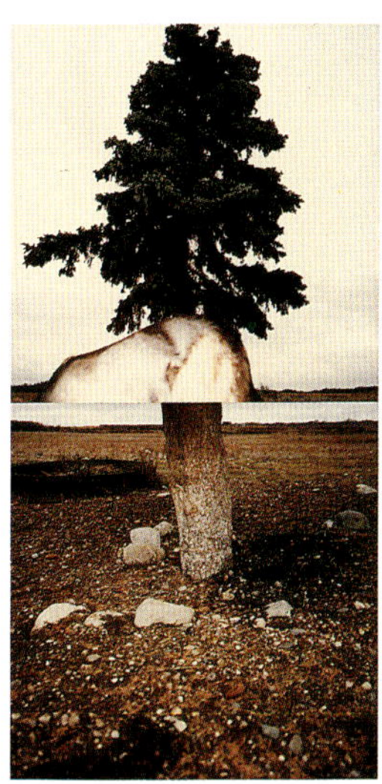

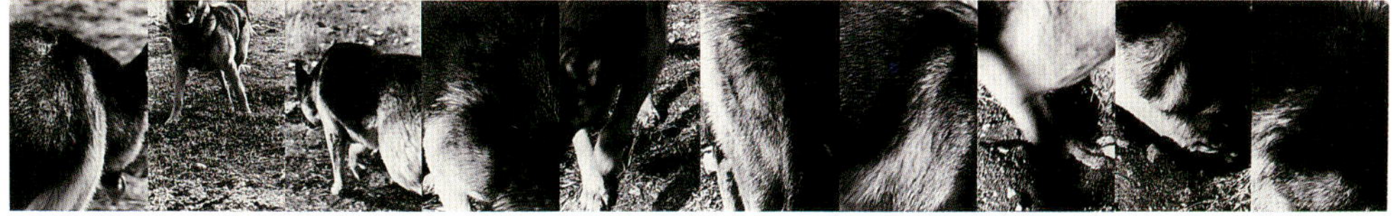

Brian Wood, *Altar*, 1980

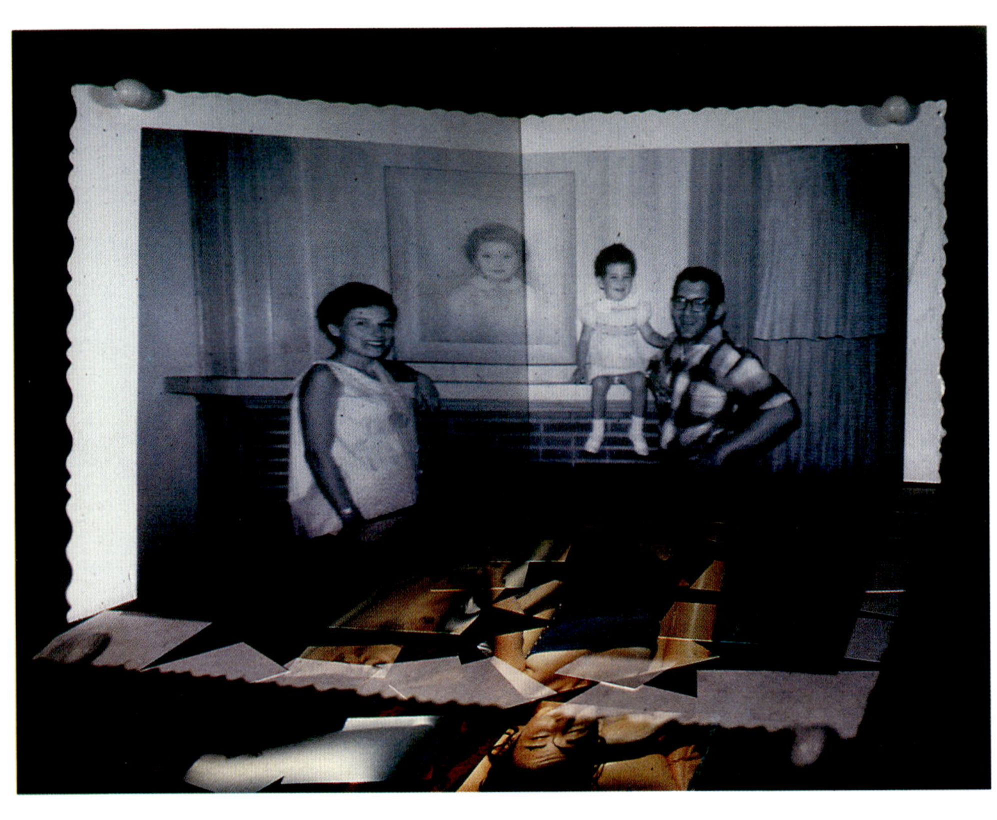

Lorie Novak, *Past Lives*, 1987

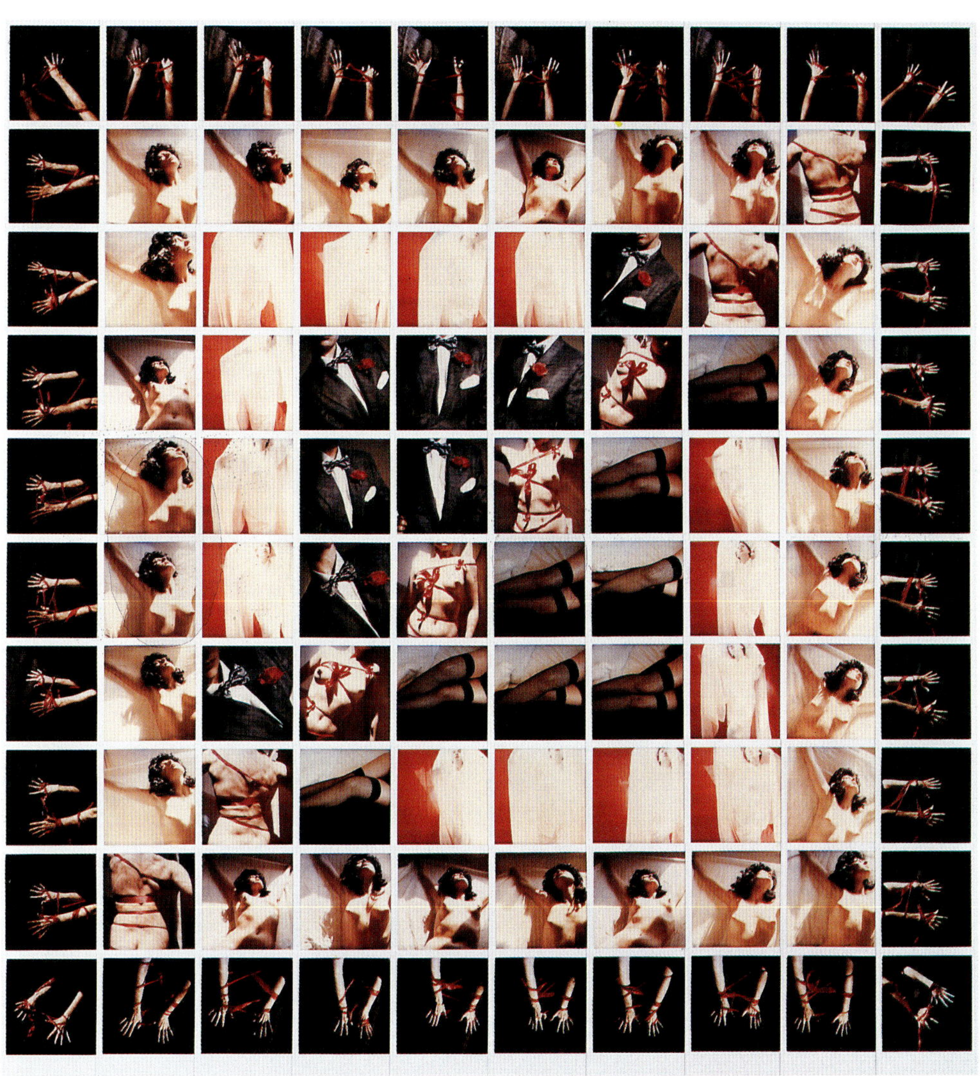

Silvia Taccani, *#97–1987*, 1987

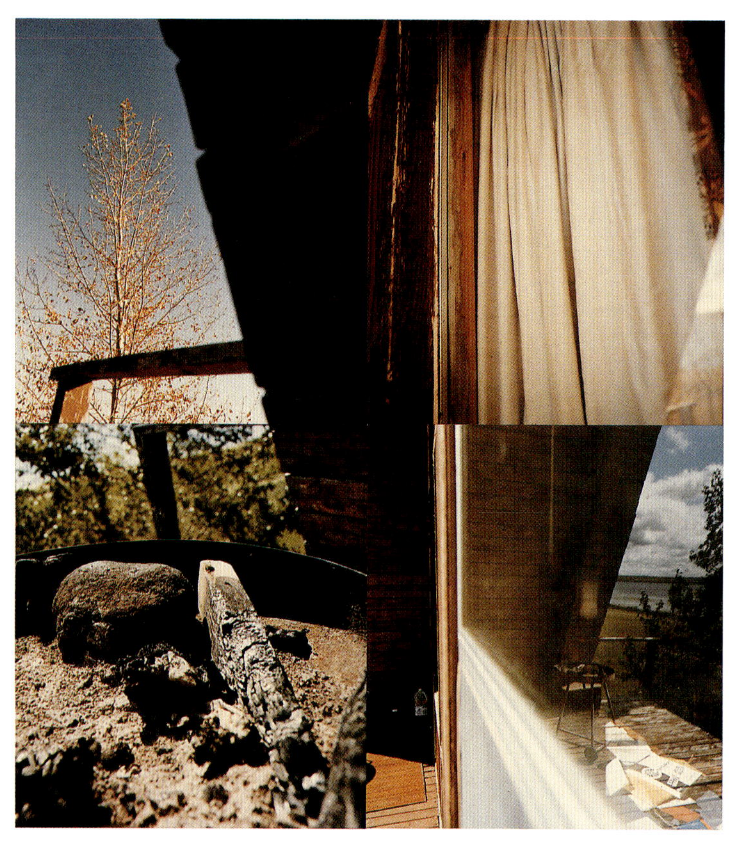

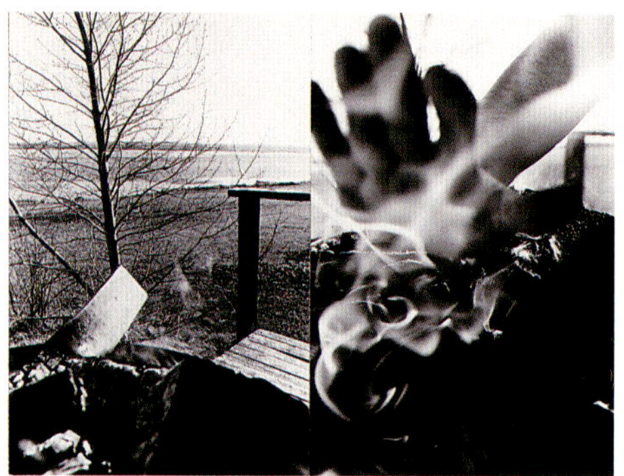

Brian Wood, *Sanctuaries*, 1980

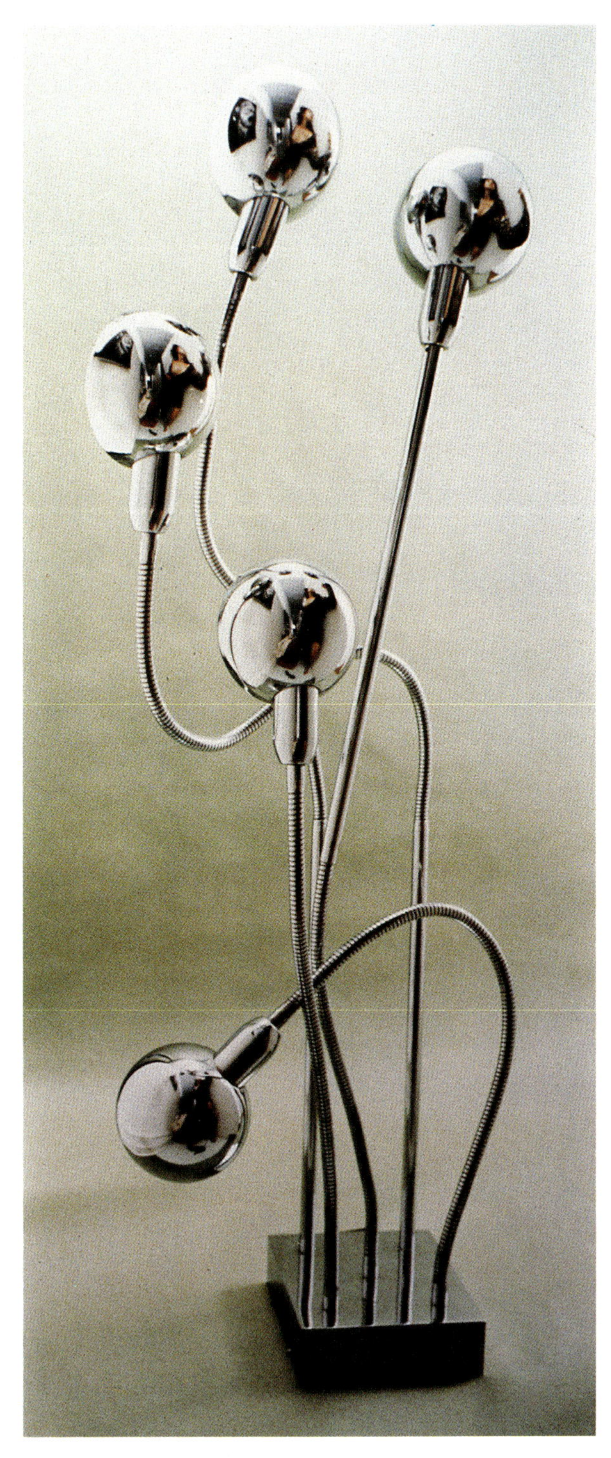

Mac Adams,
Interrogation, 1986

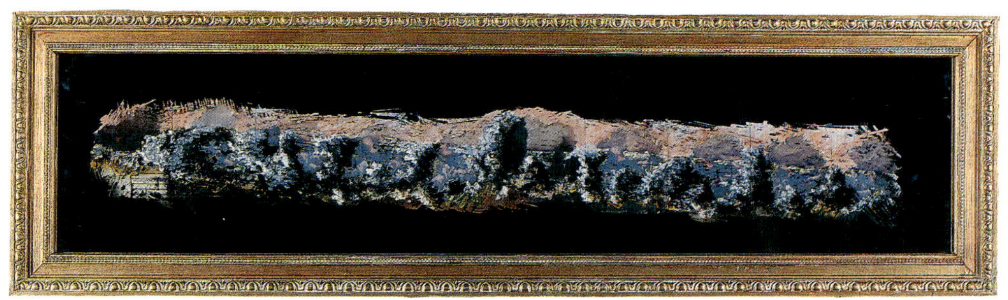

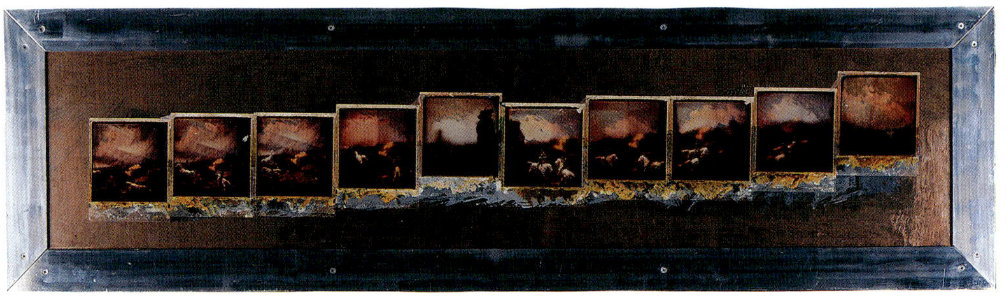

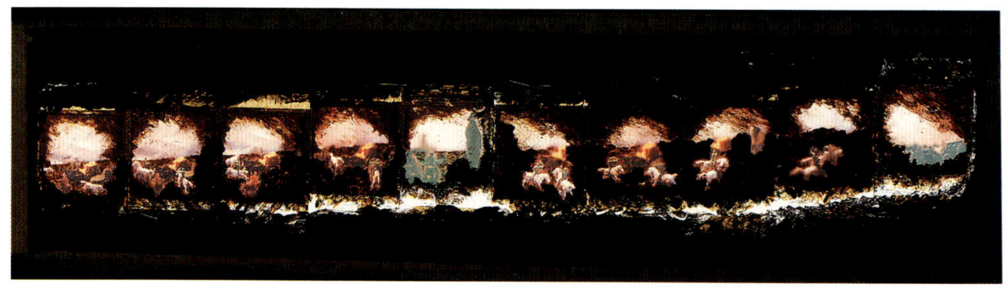

Jean-Charles Blanc, *Painted Desert*, 1983–86

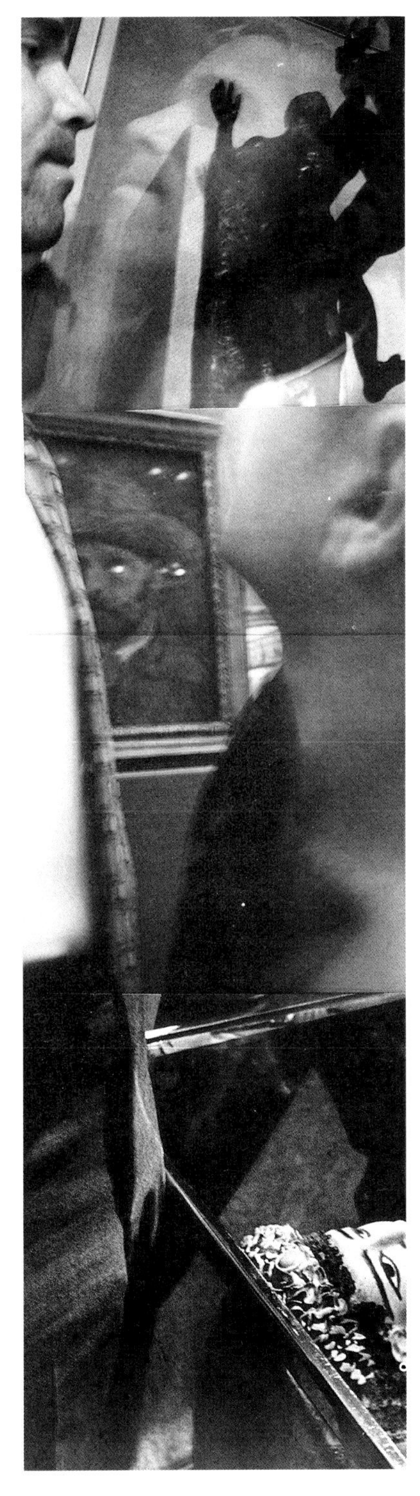

Hope Sandrow,
They Can Only Give You Answers, 1986

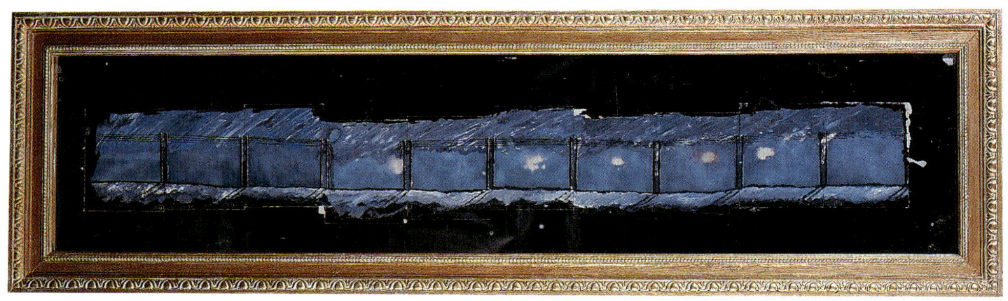

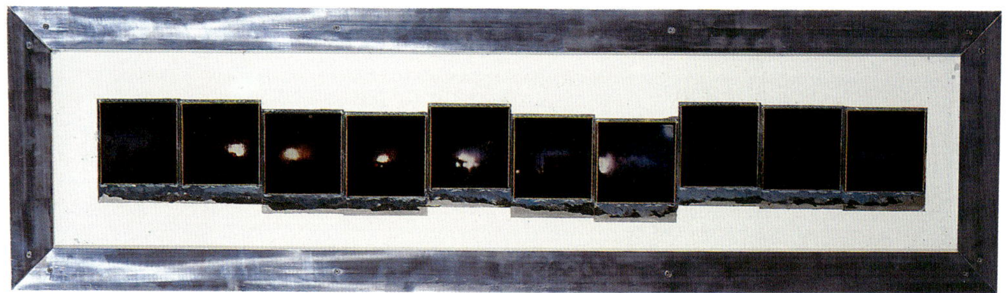

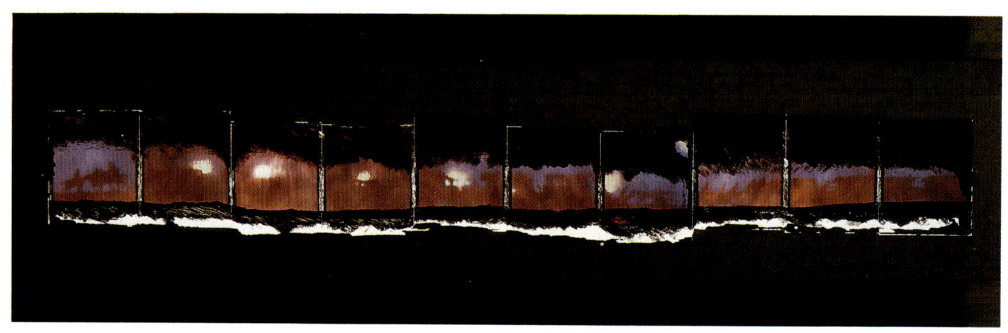

Jean-Charles Blanc, *Last News from the West*, 1983–86

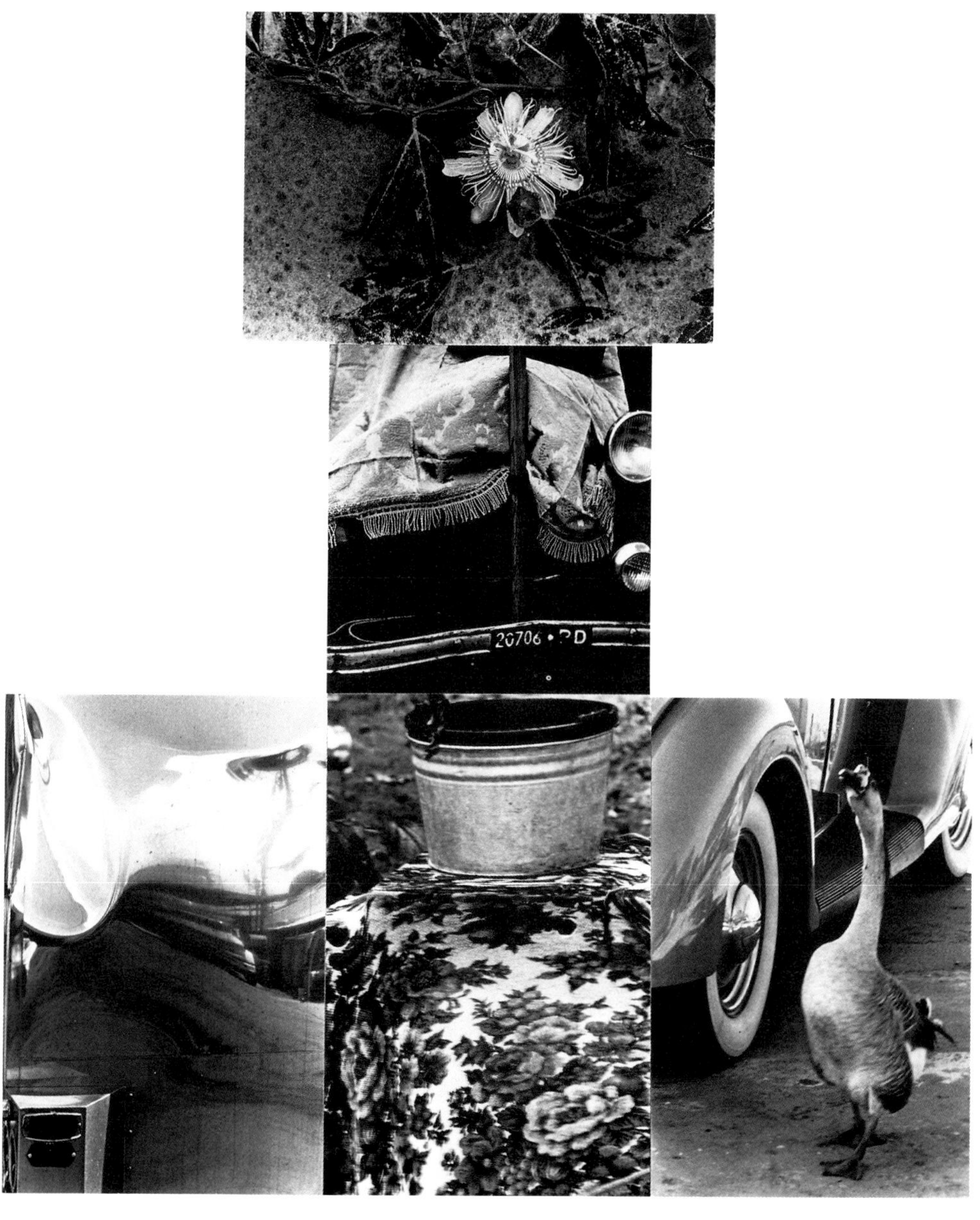

Robert Rauschenberg, *Photem Series I, no. 2*, 1981

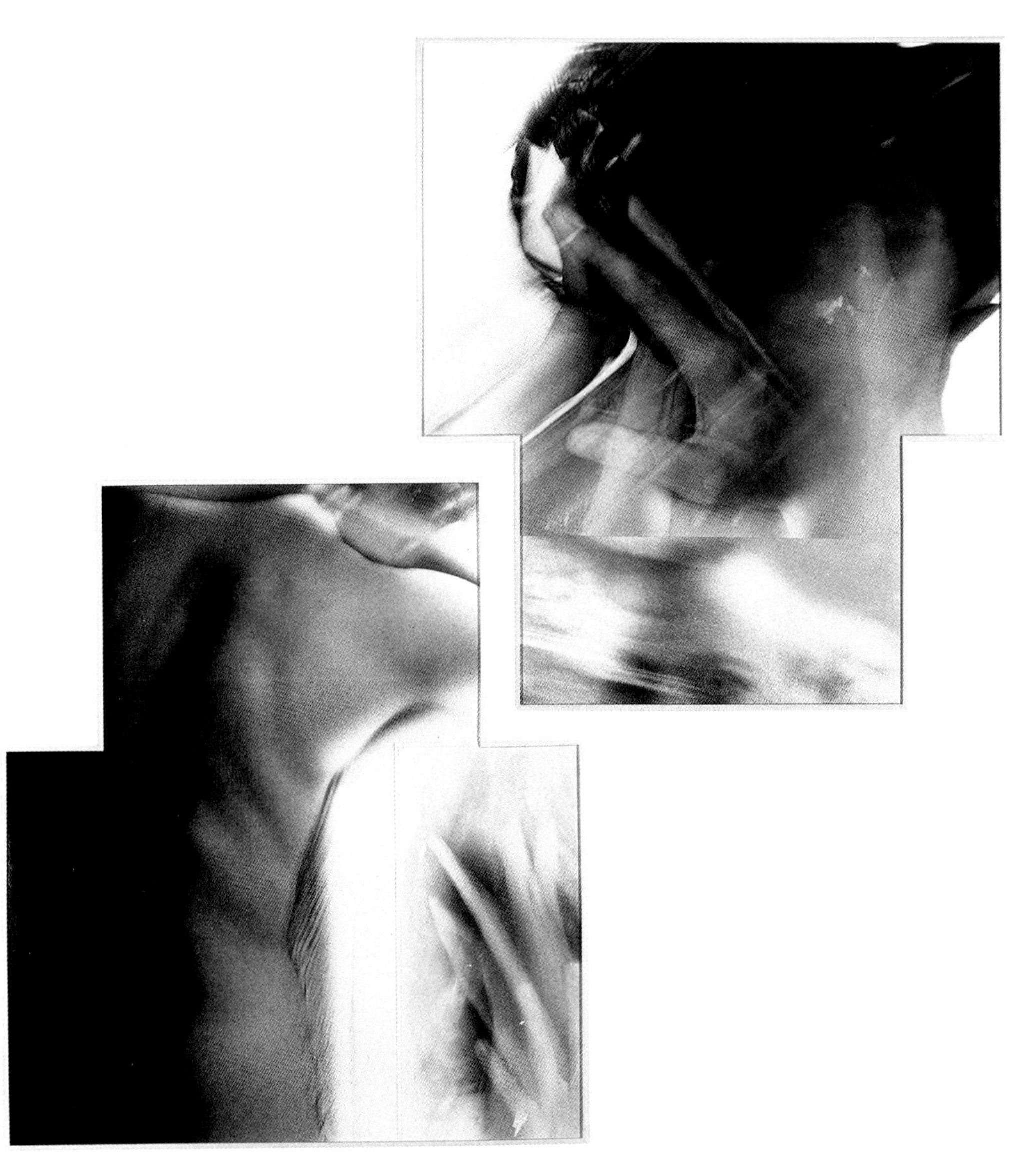

Hope Sandrow, *Measured Chaos*, 1988

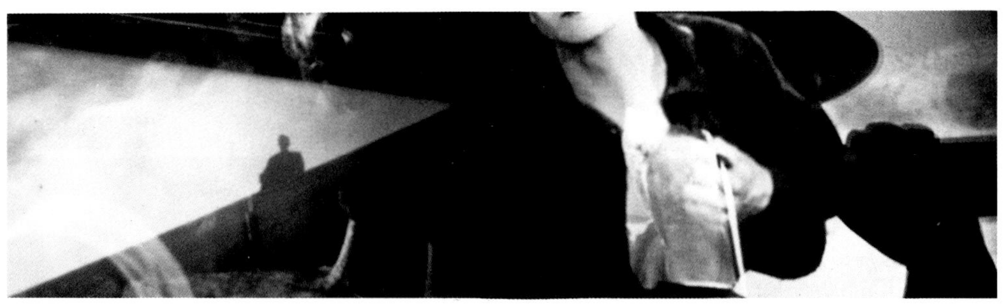

John Schlesinger, Untitled, 1988

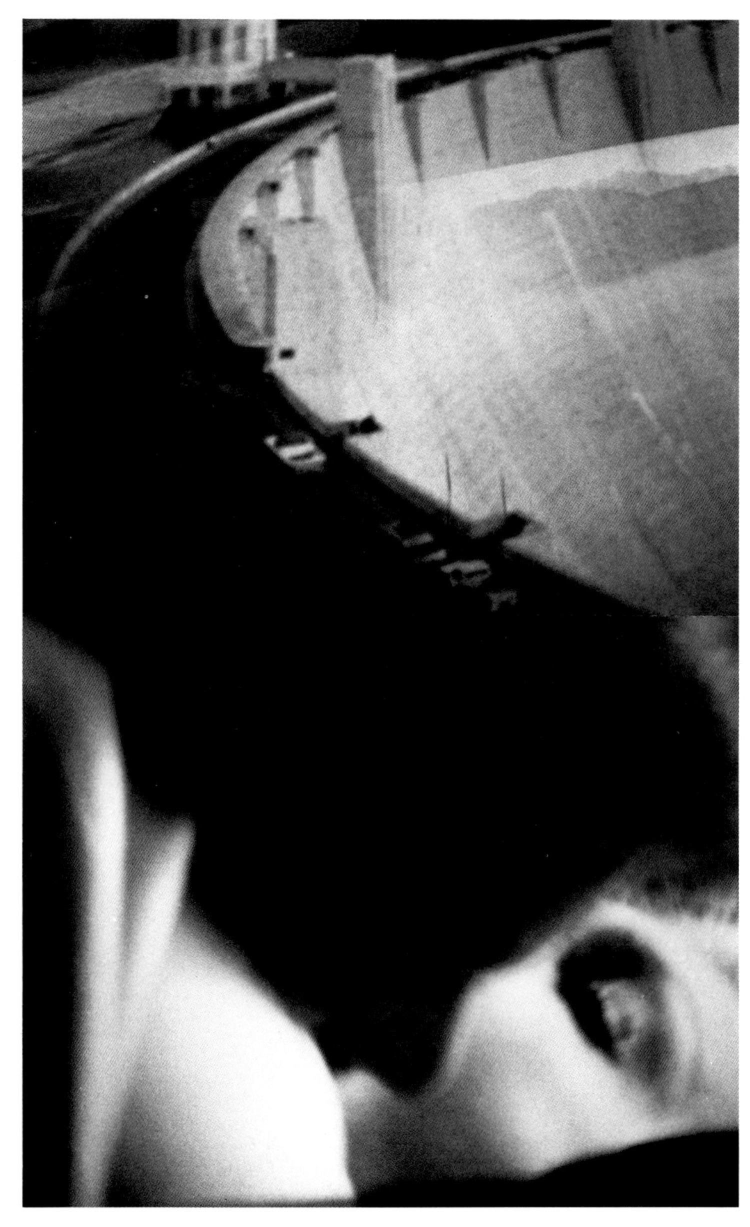

John Schlesinger, Untitled, 1987

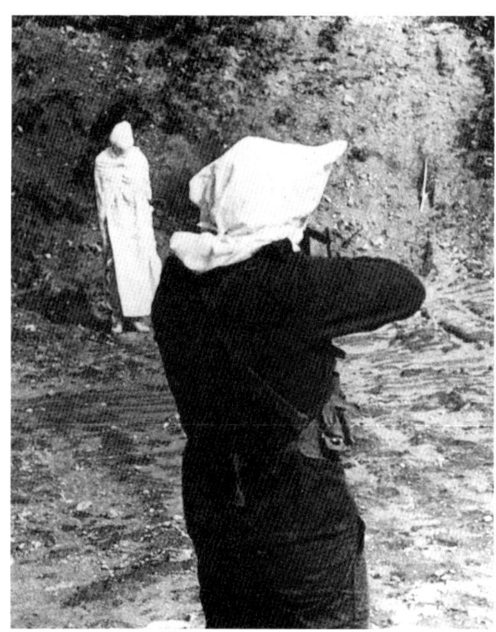

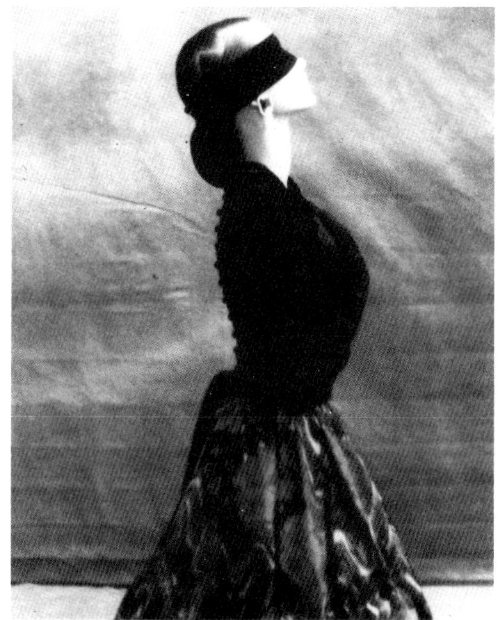

William Larson, *Lexigraphic Portrait: Moda/Grif*, 1987

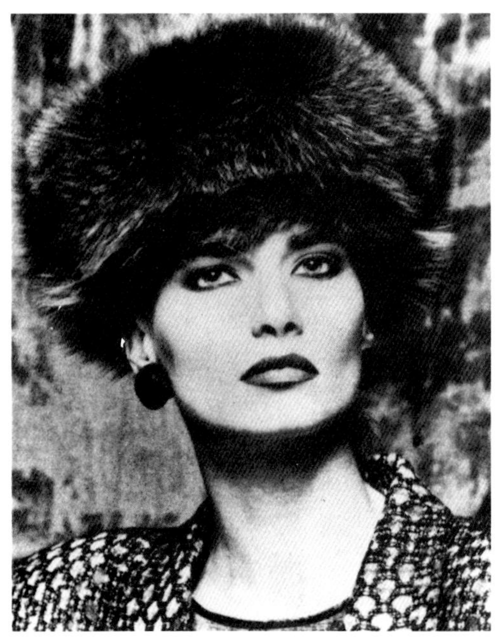

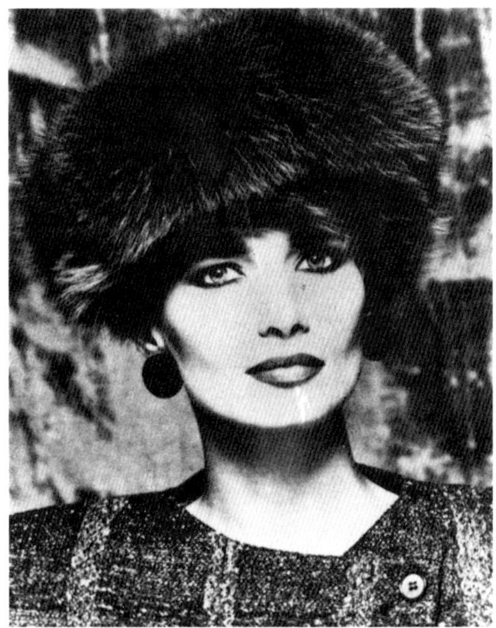

William Larson, *Lexigraphic Portrait: Newsweek/Harpers*, 1987

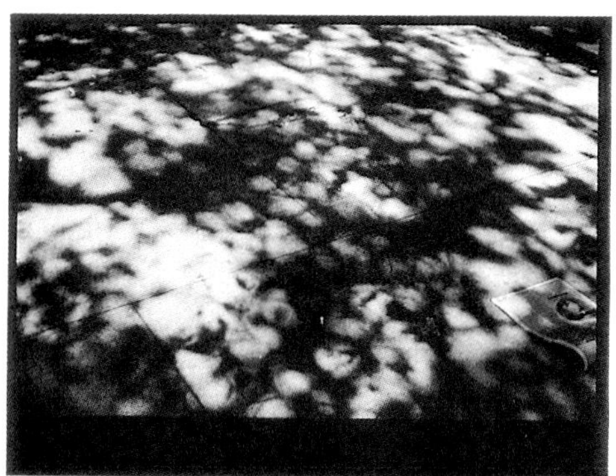
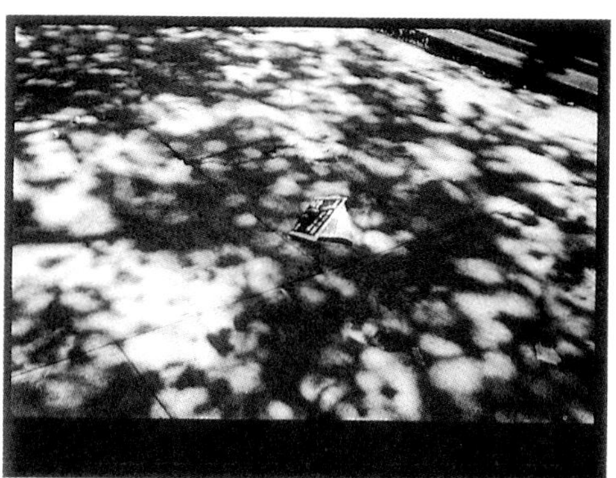

Eve Sonneman, *Newspaper, N.Y.*, 1980

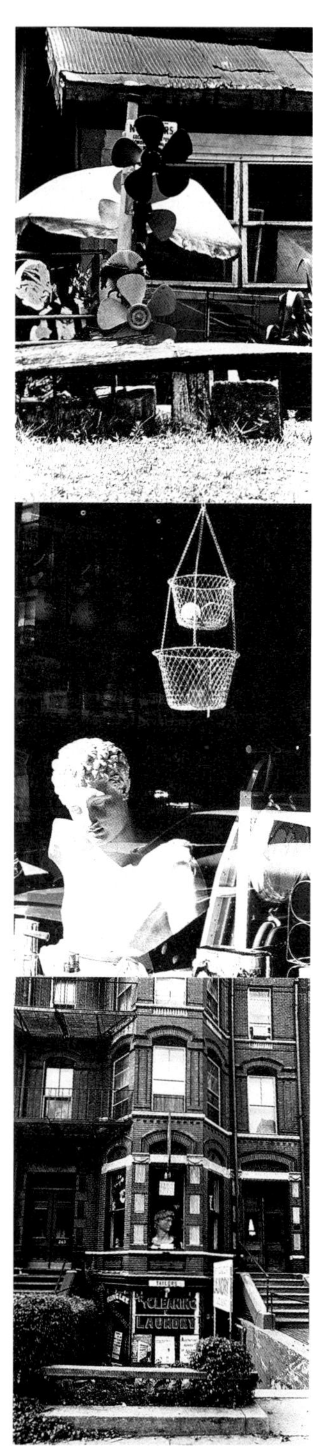

Robert Rauschenberg, *Photem Series I, no. 17*, 1981

INCONSEQUENCE AND CONSEQUENCE Eve Sonneman's diptychs (pages 45, 63) appear to offer a paradigm of ordinary vacation-photographs-relegated-to-bureau-drawer. *Starfish, Mexico,* for example, is a diptych of starfish, rocks, water, and the shadow of a head that impinges on the baseline of the photographs. In the right-hand image, the shadow becomes a bit more prominent and the starfish have moved ever so slightly. If we were to look at these pictures over the shoulder of a friend, their subject might hold some interest. Placed in their current book and gallery context, their subject loses any possible appeal. Given its banality and its appearance in temporal/spatial twos, the photographs then appear to be a paradigm of self-conscious photography; photographs "about" the taking of the photographs themselves—a situation often described, as in a 1943 short story by Lionel Trilling.

> On the lawn the peach tree was still in fruit and young Hilda Aiken was taking a picture of it. She held the camera tight against her chest. She wanted the sun behind her, but she did not want her own long morning shadow in the foreground. She raised the camera, but that did not help, and she lowered it, but that made things worse. She twisted her body to the left, then to the right. In the end she had to step out of the direct line of the sun. At last she snapped the shutter and wound the film with intense care.[1]

The camera eye has a history of solicitation. We easily imagine ourselves in its place (a position we all have at one time or another assumed). And, as we put ourselves in its place, we easily forget that the camera was ever there. *We* are there in its stead. To whatever degree this substitution of ourselves for the camera may occur, we are certain of one thing: that the *subject* of any photograph *must* have been where it was at *that* particular motionless instant.

Photographs thus encourage a fiction of our co-presence with their subjects. At the same time, we are well aware that we are not in the picture and, moreover, that the subject of the photographs is no longer exactly the way it was at the time the picture was taken. The contradictory convictions that the subject of a photograph is somehow present to us and irretrievably in another time and place give the photograph a psychic charge unlike any other kind of imagery. It is, in fact, this aspect of the photograph as a record of both presence and absence that has prompted such investments of commentary from 1839 onward.

Sonneman's photographs seem models for these kinds of solicitations, but such particularly photographic (al)lures do not become manifest. We do not care to cast ourselves in her cast shadow. Nor do we feel a poignancy for those two particular photographic moments. Our attention, if we give them any, is toward their inconsequentiality.

They do begin a sequencing we have come to expect from Eadweard Muybridge's motion studies to contemporary photo novels. But they do not continue it. We can become caught in an oscillation back and forth from one to the other, diverted from the expected logic of time to a movement in space. Stationed as they are, the pictures assume a doubly exaggerated meaningfulness (witness the extensive use of pairs in the teaching of art history and in advertising). We may strain to note the slightest variations and/or similarities from one to the other. There is little to note.

The resulting (in)(con)sequentiality flips our classroom/consumer expectations outward. We move on (perhaps in irritation), not to what can be observed in these pictures, but to what is *not* in them, to all that is not represented, the absent befores and afters and in-betweens and could have beens. These most photographic of photographs (they tell of time, of place, and of the exact position of the sunlight and of the photographer) do not behave like photographs. The inconsequentiality of their subjects (dislocated as they are from their vacation snapshot album and placed in a book and a gallery) invalidate a traditional allure, that is to say, they deliberately render useless the fiction of ourselves as being in the camera's place and the consequent poignancy of an absence.

The subject of Vikky Alexander's *Grace* (page 35), a ten-foot cross made up of photographs of Elvis Presley, unlike that of Sonneman's *Starfish*, is a subject of consequence and appears to solicit the typical photographic fiction of co-presence and the poignancy of an absence. We immediately recognize the dead rock star. We see changes from photograph to photograph. The well-known face is heavier, older, leaner, younger, smiling, anguished, sultry. But the photographs clearly are studio portraits, the head posed against neutral backgrounds. Moreover, they are oversized, extreme close-ups. There is no sense of anyone ever having actually taken them, no assumptions of camera positions. Any placings for our identifications are absent. All the same bland style, they were, in fact, taken from the covers of eight record albums. Their highly visible artifice partially nullifies the photographs' temporal and spatial incisiveness and blunts the particular poignancy of a "then," placing them more in the context of an era than of an individual life.

This primary distancing of the artifice of the studio pose is increased through its "appropriation" by Alexander, which puts the images at yet a further distance from any "contact" with their subject. They have been removed from their origins, from the act of photographing.

But perhaps it is their highly referential cruciform framing that most speaks to and, in the same gesture, most turns us away from the subject of *Grace*'s photographs. It subdues the attraction of Elvis-as-photograph. Whereas photographs establish their meaning along the axis of a physical relation to their subject—the subject *must* have been physically present for the photograph to have been made—forms such as crosses, totems, and altarpieces traditionally have signaled the nonrepresentable, that which is beyond materiality and time. As these Elvis photographs are framed into their cruciform, they become less and less their own subject. Such a frame(work) presents parallels to photography's allure of co-presence and absence while, at the same time, negating it. As with Sonneman's images, we are turned outside of the pictures themselves, along byways, perhaps ironic, humorous, sociological, ritualistic, or psychological. We move toward what Roland Barthes has termed the "mythological tissue" of mass consumer society, arriving at Pamela Zoline's encomium of a cereal box:

> On it are squandered wealths of richest colors, virgin blues, crimsons, dense ochres, precious pigments once reserved for sacred paintings and as cosmetics for the blind faces of marble gods. Giant size. Net Weight 16 ounces, 250 grams. 'They're tigeriffic!' says Tony the Tiger.[2]

From cruciform/rock star to cereal box tiger—these are the wandering substitutions encouraged by (what it is perhaps still legitimate to call) postmodern photographic practice, a practice that is intensely about photography and that, with equal intensity, subverts a photographic fiction of co-presence and the allure of a *specific* absence.

MATERIALITY AND MEMORY Jean-Charles Blanc photographs toy cowboys and Indians on table-top deserts, mountains, and valleys (pages 54, 56). He speaks of his rows of playful Polaroids as operating according to *une sorte d'attardement dérisoire*, a "ridiculous delay," which is, in part, caused by an overlapping visualization of the history of photography.

A thin layer of the Polaroids has been stripped away, making them transparent, rather than opaque. The black backing of the mirrors on which they are placed has been partially scratched off, partially painted over. The resulting play of opacity, transparency, and materiality creates a visual ambiguity and a referential array. The Polaroid, the most *au courant* mode of photographic spontaneity, becomes the reflective daguerreotype (the "mirror with a memory"), the glass collodion negative, the ambrotype positive, and reminds us of Marcel Duchamp's "Delay in Glass," his subtitle for *The Bride Stripped Bare by Her Bachelors, Even.* Duchamp's bride, in turn, traces her lineage to his *Nude Descending the Staircase*, which is linked genetically to Muybridge's and Etienne-Jules Marey's motion studies.

Painted telephone poles and railway tracks, traditional markers of an ordered space in one-point perspective that photography inherited from the Renaissance, are on the mirror/glass reverse of the rows of Polaroids. But, instead of receding toward a vanishing point, Blanc's lines run *parallel* to the frame; markers are sent askew and locations devalued.

In very different ways, Sonneman, Alexander, and Blanc have emptied the photographs of their temporal and spatial specificity. A sense of direct contact with a specific past time and place has been detoured. Walter Benjamin's photographic "tiny spark of accident"[3] has been snuffed out (the "within-timeness" of the photograph) to make room for all sorts of other accidents. Yet, in the same gesture, the identity of the images as made up of particularly photographic matter has been intensified.

We seem to be in the face of a form of postmodernisms' "problematized referent" whereby the material of the signifier (in this case photography) is favored over the meanings of the signifieds (the subjects of the photographs).

Certainly, postmodern photography is self-consciously emptying itself of its referential, signifying potential in voiding its particular spatial and temporal camera/subject attachments. Photography's traditional role of signifier-as-direct-trace is over and again invalidated.

John Maggiotto's images (pages 37, 48), all photographed from television monitors, evidence the scan lines of their origins as well as the light-sensitive photographic emulsion, toned in pinks and blue-grays, which he has applied onto thick, uneven, white plaster surfaces. The literal weight of his work fossilizes the intangible scan lines of video and transforms the usually unobtrusive materiality of the video and photographic processes into matter to be recognized, looked at. In one triptych two shards from television dramas visually blast out (a gun on the left points left, a gaze on the right looks right) from a central image of tanks taken from a newscast. In another triptych Dan Rather, lips pursed in silenced speech, a giant fragment of a face, and a video cameraman entering a building have been culled from the flicker of video and hardened into photography. A sense of the temporal/spatial "thickening" of the imagery—of an accumulated residue of television broadcasting—subverts the temporal/spatial incisiveness of the photographs and muffles their (already secondhand) attachments to their subjects.

All photographs inevitably are "thick" and culture-bound—because of their ubiquity more so than any other medium with the (historically recent) exception of television. Photography has held a long-running dialogue with its norms, a dialogue exceptionally evident during the 1960s when it spawned a multitude of images and sequences that acted as reflectors of its worldliness. Two species of dialogue (neither one completely pure of the other) were most evident: conceptualist expositions on forms of signification (such as permutation, repetition, indication, etc.—John Baldessari's pointing series of 1972–73, for example) and, second, pop gestural mimes of signification (as in Robert Rauschenberg's multimedia works). With the photographic "appropriations" of the 1980s, the conceptualist form of exposition and the pop form of visual mime merged into replication-as-commentary. Photographs increasingly were identical to those whose cultural workings they were critiquing; the only changes were the contexts in which they were placed—Sherrie Levine's photographs are the most extreme example of this. In all cases (conceptual, pop, appropriation) the photographic image was, in theory at least, detached from any direct relationship to its actual subject—its referent—and related to the multiple comings and goings and repositionings *of* that subject.

But the terms are changing.

In Gretchen Bender's *Total Recall* (page 38), from a five-by-eight-foot steel armature, three vertical slivers of filmstrip beam forth fluorescent images, some of computer generated abstract shapes and corporate logos, others identifiable fragments of television narratives, commercials, and newscasts.

As is the case with Maggiotto's pictures, all of Bender's images are photographed from video screens. Many, however, are less recognizable than his, having been manipulated to the edge of legibility through numerous video and film techniques. Set as they are in their formidable armature (not coincidentally, almost all new computer art forms had their origins in military research), the *Total Recall* stills convey a powerful sense of never-ending connections, contacts, continuities, feedbacks, interface, and circuities, all of which we can never completely grasp.

Total Recall visualizes "an electronically introduced hyperperception" and, as Jonathan Crary has commented, changes in human perception from which there is no going back.[4] The capabilities of information-communication technology are far beyond that of any human response. The gap between our senses and the fast pace of the media is unbridgeable. We are always at a lag. These hyperactive changes re-situate the present (and ourselves as inhabiting the present) as already within a past, historical moment.

The title, *Total Recall*, originally was suggested by a 1966 Phillip K. Dick science fiction story, "We Can Remember It for You Wholesale," whose protagonist undergoes several "extra-factual memory implants" designed to both erase old memories and provide new ones of previously unknown, and conceivably non-existent, places, persons, and situations. Bender's *Total Recall* materializes an electronic form of that synthetic memory. Implanted in their wall of brushed steel, juxtapositions of artificial electronic images (images without an original referent), newscast snippets, advertising logos, and the like, almost become interchangeable. The often barely recognizable images are questionable photographic markers of subjects that may or may not have ever existed—potentially they are all markers of nonpresences, nontimes, nonplaces and of immaterial, artificially generated futures.

The performance version of *Total Recall* is a stage of multiple television monitors, many of them screening identical images. The plurality of televisions generates a sense of negation and absence, becoming a sort of nonsite that Jonathan Crary has related to Robert Smithson's work with mirrors within landscapes in the late 1960s.[5] Smithson's paradoxical mirror placements caused his sites to be displaced or negated by the very material objects (mirrors) that constituted them.

Although the project of a nonsite is contrary to photography as a reflexive medium, given the necessity of a presence for the very existence of its imagery, the difference is that the landscapes photography now reflects are often at a double or triple or multiple remove and some may never have existed in any place or time.

It is no longer a question of a *photographic* absence/presence; that is, the photograph as the present, material trace of an absent, past moment. Rather, the presence of the images themselves is increasingly emphatic—thickened and layered and multiplied and blown up in size—while their connections to that which they configure is increasingly distanced by their multiple repositionings and, ultimately, by the increasingly fragile materiality of their origins.

In the early nineteenth century, when railroads first appeared, there was an attempt to control the disruptions incurred by the revolution in travel. Passengers were sometimes given *garde vue*,[6] blinders against the disorientation of the new speed of travel. Around the same time, the invention of photography provided another form of the *garde vue*, the *aide mémoire*, a guard against the flood of new and old sights. Postmodern photography can no longer be on guard—except, perhaps, against its own disorientations. What possibly might be considered travel photography can no longer be its own genre.

The photographic projections layering Nancy Goldring's *The Traveler Remembers* (pages 43, 44) are ghosts of their former lives. Transparent, fragile, on the edge of immateriality, they speak to the elusive, mutating function of an *aide mémoire* in which photography can no longer be enlisted.

Connections are lost in delicate layerings, photography becomes a *perte de vue*.

The projections hover over and within grid formations. Like many postmodern photographic uses of the grid, Goldring's grid accents rather than subdues a spatialization of time, emphasizing the grid's diagrammatical functions. The possible horizontal, vertical, and diagonal orders that work contrary to a sequential temporality are encouraged. Photographic time and space, as it is slotted into such emphatic orderings assumes the quality of temporal/spatial intersections—intersections accentuated in *The Traveler Remembers* by the diagonals of light shaft, tabletop, and moldings that visually crisscross from frame to frame. The time/space suggested by Goldring's intersecting variables is different from the sense of hyperperceptual flow of Bender's *Total Recall* and different from the sense of condensation suggested by the work of Blanc or of thickness suggested by the materiality of Maggiotto's pictures, or the frictions/fusions of time/place/body suggested by the cruciform.

Goldring writes of her work as presenting "insubstantial evidence with convincing precision."[7] The terms can just as easily be reversed: convincing evidence with insubstantial precision. The photograph's function of materializing a moment of the outer world has been put to the task of representing an inner psychological space as if it were an outwardly projected one. From a raised platform the immobile "traveler," her doubled shadows larger than her body, looks out a small window onto an unchanging mountain view. Below, the gray crowds (from Grand Central Station) remain constant from frame to frame. It is behind her, where she is *not* looking, that the scenery changes. Figures at a table of unwritten pages alternate with tabled fields and plains. And, always at the traveler's back, a huge gridded window unmarks changes of scenery—insubstantial dioramas of memory.

Acutely photographic, *The Traveler Remembers* records the unphotographic postmodern condition of *perte de mémoire*. But perhaps, rather than a loss of memory, it is still a question of a relocation; a displacement of one kind of memory so as to make a space for others.

TRANSUBSTANTIATION AND METAMORPHOSIS Brian Wood's *Sanctuaries* and *Altar* (pages 49, 52), join various sites (or different views of the same site—it is impossible to know) so that their vertical and lateral connections form unitary objects as well as diverse spaces—a movement opposite to contemporary proto-Cubist photographic assemblages that fragment one site. A place is made into a new unchartable thing/place.

The terms of place are changing. Spatializations that have located people and discourses are breaking down. There is, to borrow Donna Haraway's phrase, a "fraying of previously secure places."[8] *Sanctuaries*, its barren "No Trespassing" land(s) above its prowling guard dog(s) signal the uncertainties of demarcations. Singularities and pluralities are lost in conjunctions. They all are within a formal configuration—the altarpiece—which signals two mutually exclusive worlds, that of the nonrepresentable and that of its representation, even as it brings them in touch.

Within photography, persons and places traditionally have come into their meanings in different ways. A photographed person must have been within a particular moment in time. Photographs of them easily have become markers of our own mortal chronology, whereas sites have been chronologized more indirectly through habitation and use by bodies. Photographs of unknown places have existed in forms of the conjectural: what it might have been like or what it could be like to be there. And known places have been populated by our absent selves, by our once having been there. Such distinctions are no longer at issue.

The deep perspective of the "No Trespassing" sign is abruptly terminated, a spatial marker we cannot follow. The imaginary illusion provided by a one-point perspective of a center of consciousness capable of looking out on the world, apprehending its structure and processes and representing them to itself as having formal coherency, is met with a terminating edge. Distinctions between body and place also are blurred, in the instance of Brian Wood's *Altar* literally so, as an out-of-focus, light-shafted hand forms one of its panels.

Dorit Cypis's *Love After Death: Anatomy Lesson* (page 34)—three large photographs each with three smaller inserts below—also recalls altarpieces and their predelle. In the primary pictures, bound within the formal conflations of the Christian story of birth, death, and transubstantiation, Cypis has layered images of body parts—hands and limbs, and vulva-like shapes glistening in the photographed slither of their organicity. In the predella panels a detail of a Bruges painting, Rembrandt's *Anatomy Lesson of Dr. Tulp*, and a female anatomy model each are flanked by details of bodies and faces taken from old photographs of Cypis's grandparents.

Here, it is the body that is primary as both site and non-site, its spaces uncertain. An arm reaches out from an improbable within. A central vulva/mandala shape is actually a larynx, substitutions based on ideological as well as formal collapses. It is through the larynx that the voice passes, that articulation occurs. Cypis's image conflates sexuality, spirituality, and vocal articulation into one and the same form. Such a collapse is indicative of a kinesthetic approach to cognition, whereby the primary models of both a linguistic structure and a psychoanalytic one are being questioned by investigations of how the body receives and stores information.[9]

Questioned also is the priority of sight: what cannot be seen and explained can, in principle, be understood. As do Wood and Alexander, Cypis places such a conflation within the context of a religious form, a form of demarcation between substance and insubstantiality, neither and both. *Love After Death* visualizes a place/nonplace where articulated language *is*, not becomes, also another language and where a body is and is not corporeal. And where a photograph is strenuously referential (many people find these images shocking and repugnant) and just as strenuously detached through an accretion of associations, many of which we cannot name.

Like Bender's *Total Recall*, Cypis's *Love After Death* is a culled marker of a performance project. In its "live" version, images directly projected onto a room's surfaces and through scrims were intercepted by the bodies of performers and spectators. Interreflections of "real" and projected time-and-space rendered bodies, memories, histories, and credos, simultaneously and chronologically absent and present.

A postmodern transubstantiation? One at a parallel remove from the uncertain boundaries between the substantial and the insubstantial of today's media themselves: photography, cinema, video?

Most of John Schlesinger's combined photographs (pages 59, 60) are taken from movie screens and are images of the psychic transubstantiations that occur as cinematic viewings lose their distinctions. A flood-shoring dam swoops to male head, architecture becomes corporeal, sexual, becomes a dark, male profile nestled within a light, female embrace. In a double-exposure, a faceless woman holds in her hand the faint, uneven light of a male head. Whether vertical or horizontal, Schlesinger's photographs provoke an inward penetration of two disparate images into one gesture, place, and time. A pointed shaft of light from one image is aimed toward a woman's throat in another. Conjoining becomes visual action, a thrusting. Paralleling the dream work of condensation, the experience of time and space in Schlesinger's juxtapositions is obliterated by the pressures of a simultaneity. The images are like mental thaumatropes; they combine to produce a single picture, a "being with" that results in metamorphosis rather than development or comparison or any other form of being "beside." The photograph's direct routes in time and space are looped astray as are the logic of their positionings. The linear, narrative reading that a horizontal format encourages and the hierarchical orderings implied by the vertical are both subsumed within the hybrid conditions of their interpenetration.

Also subsumed are the basic assumptions about spatial equilibrium that the vertical and horizontal connote. The figure within a circle within a square of Leonardo da Vinci's rendering of the Vetruvian schema indicates not only the ideal proportions of man as a measure of all things; the polarities of left/right and top/bottom also address the psychological state of his upright stance. Accordingly, we enter Renaissance paintings and their photographic derivatives on *terra firma*.

The postmodern (sub)versions of photographic *terra firma* (it is never a question of when or where the camera was) are achieved, not by denying photography its "look," but through an insistence upon the ways its imagery may coalesce and dissipate. As such, they refer to the intensity of the surrogate visual experience (in Schlesinger's case, cinematic and photographic). Like Maggiotto's plaster shards or Blanc's Polaroids, fictions and histories are confounded.

INTERROGATION AND THE SELF Called into question is the control—temporal, spatial, and psychological—exerted by a supposed photographic "reality"—its direct connection to its subject—and the ways in which this "reality" has been put to the service of apparently logical juxtapositions and sequences. This is a central issue in photographic praxis today that speaks not only to aesthetics, but to the ideologies of moral control that all closed systems connote.

In the catalogue *Serial Imagery* to what has been considered a landmark exhibition of 1968, John Coplans wrote: "The [serial] approaches of the artists mentioned above [ranging from Monet to Mondrian to Warhol and Stella] in no small measure evoke the underlying control-systems central to an advanced, 'free-enterprise' technological society."[10]

Timerman's Dream, by Klaus Schnitzer and Robert Sennhauser (page 46), is a grid of photographs, the first left image an entrance, the last right image an exit. The strongly perspectival pictures seem a perfectly ordered photographic view and, unlike Sonneman's pictures, a completed paradigm of the photo-narrative.

Schnitzer and Sennhauser have described the individual shots, left to right, as follows:

> (1) entrance into a building; (2) information; (3) isolation; (4) doctors/inquisitors? (5) passage; (6) interrogation; (7) bodily harm? (8) passage; (9) interrogation; (10) death (spiritual/physical?); (11) passage; (12) doctors/inquisitors? (13) isolation; (14) information; (15) exit.[11]

Immediately apparent are the reiteration of doubt (bodily harm? spiritual/physical? doctors/inquisitors?) and four sets of doublings. As visualized, these doublings flicker the three superimposed rows in and out of a grid form. They are positioned along a central, vertical line and two diagonals, forming an asterisk, a set of visual intersections that erupt amid the linear flow from the entrance to the exit frames of *Timerman's Dream*, both connecting and raying out its components from their sequential mode.

Read linearly, the four doublings also are disruptive. A sequence originates out of a need to go beyond a repetitive form: it operates as a process of becoming, the becoming of meaning, a higher order of relation than that of a repetition. Experientially, a repetition is the necessary confirmation that defines a thing or event as other than isolated.

When, as in *Timerman's Dream*, a repetitive doubling occurs in a sequence, the sense of confirmation that it articulates in experience mutates. The doublings signal an infinite number of repetitions, recalling the tortures and inquisitions of its nominal subject from Jacobo Timerman's book *Prisoner Without a Name, Cell Without a Number.* If/and referring to the photographic act of doubling (analogous to Blanc's mirrors), repetition signals the punctuation of the dream—Timerman's—by the "real time" of the mechanical setup. And repetitions signal the echoing temporalities and spatialities of mass production and mass consumption of the photograph as reportage.

Whatever the visual reflections may be, the simple temporal progression from entrance to exit is intersected and slivered by repetition. These sliverings set up intersecting photographic instances, routing their subject away from the direct temporal and spatial cuts of the photographic toward the uncertain mappings of pose, dream, and media times and spaces—all reflections of the photographic as dis-played in the certain fullness of its suggested doubts.

In one frame (no. 10), a cloth dummy substitutes for a body, thus deputizing all the other (already questionable in their identities) bodies. In their reflexive interchangeability locations and persons are absent and present, sites and non-sites.

Mac Adams's *Interrogation* and *Trapped* (pages 47, 53) picture staged scenes of violence repeatedly mirrored in shiny objects, literal reflections of the photograph's repetitive mirroring of an instant in time—a mirroring that becomes distorted in its repeated reflexivity. But, the temporality of Mac Adams's "moments" also is inextricably linked to that of the genre he mimics. His are reflections of and on the culminating pivot of a narrative, specifically that of mystery or crime stories read primarily for distraction. Such distraction is predicated on a development of events so familiar that there is a withdrawal from the tension of past-present-future and a focus on an *instant*, anticipated, desired, and rewarded. The time of the mystery instant is different from the time of the photographic instant. It is the instant of always-the-same-story, its consolation predicated on the "return of the Identical,"[12] which meets the photographic instant in the tension of the past, of the that-which-never-will-return. Yet again, the blatant artificiality of Mac Adams's setups partially redirects a photographic temporality and spatiality toward the more generalized time of an era and a genre, meeting, as it were, his subject half way. Photography, in Mac Adams's work, is subsumed into its secondary referent—that of its genre or norm.

Dennis Adams's *Ba(bb)le: Podium for Dissent* (pages 39, 40) provides another address to photographic iteration. A tall structure (its planned height is forty-four feet), its five tilted, rectangular boxes with illuminated photographs create a laddered cinematic progression of expression and gesticulation at the intersections of art, architecture, advertising, and news media.[13] *Ba(bb)le* illustrates the skewered repetitiveness of photographic reproduction and, like Mac Adams's *Interrogation* and *Trapped*, Dennis Adams's use of photographic repetition also is reflexive of his genre—political and media campaigns.

Similar to mystery stories and other genres of distraction, the reiteration of *Ba(bb)le* as campaign (a reiteration upon which campaigns depend) calls upon the comfort of the foreseen and the known reappearance. But a "return of the Identical" is no longer possible. Although *Ba(bb)le*'s images are the same, they are framed and angled differently and, therefore, not the same. The ways in which the frame sets up the subject and the subject the frame are tilted, skewered, and inelegant. They imply both progress and repetition while being neither one nor the other. The cropped and recropped unknown place and moment of the pose are everyone's and no one's place and moment.

The function of a podium, a form for the literal elevation of verbal address, for the raising of the authority of the speaker, is undermined. In a different way from Cypis's *Love After Death*, the functions of speech and bodies are called into play. As viewers, we have to get down on our hands and knees to see all the photographs. Viewer positionings are deliberate in this and other Dennis Adams' works to explore, in his words, "how the entire body comes to terms with information, not just the eyes and the mind."[14] The photographic allure of time and place has been replaced by one of utility. Dennis Adams uses, in his words, "the image of utility as a decoy or lure."[15]

While recalling the insistent visual scatter of mass campaigns, in its vertical structure of grinning faces, *Ba(bb)ble* also recalls the forms of the totemic. This association with "invested forms" symbolic of existing conventions, of a *being* of meaning, exists along with and in contradiction to the narcissistic refraction of meaning intimated by *Ba(bb)le*'s fluorescent photographic echoes of an unknown smile for unseen audiences.

Dennis Adams thinks of his work as a kind of "pure advertising" whose goal is to capture attention through a disregard for its own product as its audience is drawn through seductive layers of images and texts. Adams wants to take this idea to its limit—toward, as he has said, "the obsolescence of the product—the subject."[16]

The fragile identities of the subjects of advertising and news photographs as they are displaced and relocated forms a central theme of William Larson's *Lexigraphic Portraits. Newsweek/Harpers Bazaar* (page 61) pictures two blindfolded conditions: a prisoner up for execution and a high-fashion model. The two contaminate each other. Killing time/place/action is pulled into pose time/place and back again, but the forces are not equal. The fashion "shot," which can be read as playful pin-the-tail-on-the-donkey or blindman's buff, becomes an unexpected assassination by proximity, a degenerate sadomasochistic *frisson* of high chic. The execution, on the other hand, does not assume the *insouciance* of its temporary partner. Associations multiply: war games, campaigns, advertising campaigns. The two parallel scenes maintain and lose their separate identities. The blindfolded subject rebounds out to the absent gaze of the unknown photographers; a paradigm for the loss of the very condition of the image's existence: the photographer's gaze.

> Advertising seems to have a life of its own; it exists in and out of other media, and speaks to us in a language we can recognize but a voice we can never identify. This is because advertising has no "subject." . . . People who produce advertising . . . are unknown and faceless, the ad in any case does not claim to speak from them. . . . Thus there is a space, a gap left where the speaker should be . . . we are drawn in to fill the gap, so that we become both listener and speaker, subject and object.[17]

Moda/Grif (page 62) shows the same model in two similar poses, excerpted from different magazine locations, raising other questions of identities and their loss. Larson's unknown model is almost, but not, identical, the same and not the same, a product of the anonymous voice-over of authority of messages sent into the public domain.

Questions of identity and placement are also articulated within the context of a more private domain, as in the photographs by Lorie Novak (pages 36, 50).

Fragments presents a perfectly articulated perspectival space, but it is not the space within the photographs themselves, rather it is that of the walls and floor onto which they have been projected. We are in a space both of and other than that of her subjects. These subjects are yet further removed by the white frame of one of the photographs and the pushpins that secure it to yet a different wall from that onto which it has been projected.

Within *Fragments* is a photograph of Novak as a young girl, seated on a mantle between her standing parents, next to a painted portrait of herself. Out of this family triad, along a dark space of floorboards, float starwars-galaxy pieces of photographed bodies: flat bits of a young man and woman, themselves floating more prosaically on rubber rafts in water.

Illusions are constantly counteracted by interruptions, overlaps posited as alternatives to organic models of growth with harmony, unity, closure.

In *Fragments*, such overlays speak to photography within the calendar of the family album. Family poses, other than occasions within flux, become matter within pictures as overlaid by other pictures. Locations disrupt a logical narrative of family album, addressing the elusive psychological conjunctions of an immaterialized camera.

Novak's *Past Lives* is also composed of projections onto a corner. Three images are visibly projected in overlaps against walls and onto gray floorboards: Novak as a child in her mother's arms, the face of Ethel Rosenberg, and a picture of children who eventually were deported to Nazi concentration camps. These three projections have a different grain, according to their sources of reproduction. In the extremity of its enlargement, the face of Ethel Rosenberg has reverted back to the grainy state of a print, visually no longer a photograph. The images of the children have undergone less use and amplification, but they are de-formed by their many re-placings. The clarity of the mother and child is muted by their overlapped positionings within orderings that had once been external. There is also a fourth, unseen projection. The central figures are colored by another projected image whose subject (Novak herself as an adult) is invisible, save for the traces of blue and flesh tones it has put out on loan to the other bodies and faces. The photographer is rendered visible (seeing herself in the third person) and invisible *within* her own subject.

As is the case with Cypis and Bender, Novak's photographs are the stilled versions of a "real" time project, in Novak's case, a four-carousel slide "performance" of overlaps and dissolves. In the slide project (and in other photographs) the same images are used and reused in differing conjunctions, dissolves, and overlaps. In one instance, Novak re-places her own mother by dissolve, becoming her own past and future.

Novak's pictures both amplify and subvert a photographic identity of the self through the repeated replications of the family archive and an historical archive. The Polaroids by (and of) Silvia Taccani (pages 42, 51) approach a different aspect of the self in the postmodern world of photographic multiplicities.

91–1987 (the titles, all numerical, refer to the year and order of their production) shows Taccani's photographed personas in various poses. Expressions are clichés and, at the same time, undefined. Doubt? Dismay? In one image, she screams. Trapped in plasticized yellow, she flits a flimsy skirt in and out of numerous waxy poses. *97–1987* is composed of squares of black-netted legs, nude torsos and arms bound in red ribbon and, the same torso, in elegant men's clothing. Other images are dramatically female: bare breasts, head flung back, arm outstretched, a possible revival of a nineteenth-century *étude pour artistes.* Poses are repeated—thirty or more times—but are never identical. Because they are Polaroids, each shot required a re-assumption of the approximate pose or mood.

All these moods and bodies that both are, and are not, Taccani are patterned into colors and shapes reminiscent of quilts or tiles or kaleidoscopic reflections. The multiple re-assumptions of women's roles and moods intersect within the reference of abstract decoration. Bodies and moods also become uncertain objects. Patterning (often considered a woman's work) is put to the service of spatializing women's guises and, in the same gesture, through the use of the photograph, maintaining an artificial "then" of the pose and a reference to the "real" then of the woman assuming the pose.

Taccani's use of the patterned grid, created by the colors and shapes of her illuminated self, makes designs that all work against content without obliterating it. Signifieds become interchangeable in patterning, double and triple losses of photographic distinctions. Taccani's displacements (she is an Italian living in the USA) are configured into a diagrammatical unity which is not a place, not totally an object, but another form of non-site. A male/female difference that could be construed hierarchically is abstracted to a difference that is visually relational.

Taccani's poses speak to Alexander's *Obsession* (page 41), a row of appropriated photographs of the model Christie Brinkley in and out of various poses, clothing, and assumed moods. Again, the nature of the commercial photographed pose sets the images into a temporality that is genre- or culture-specific rather than individual. This mitigates the incisiveness of the photographic gesture and mutes any reading as a temporal progression. The progression suggested by the linearity of *Obsession* is denied further by its right to left numbering, which counters the Western viewer's reading habits and exceptions.

With one exception (no. 3 where two photographs of different sizes are joined to form one Brinkley figure), *Obsession* is a sequence of interchangeable variables without interruptions, repetitions, or expectations. Its seemingly infinite variability of gesture and pose and mood, and seemingly infinitely possible substitutions of faces and bodies, which the habitual uses of photography have created, gives new meaning to the variations that come into play. The pictures of Christie Brinkley are part of a particular cultural time and place within the histories of fashion, advertising, and the general commodification of Western woman. Yet, in their endless variability, almost, but not actually repetitive, they also give a sense of another kind of time, a cyclical time. There is a sense of gesture, an event that will recur repeatedly, the sameness of its reoccurrence overriding any differences in the configurations of its return.

The notion of the "return," related to that of a photographic temporal/spatial solicitation, is an idea central to a photographic tradition that, in postmodern practice, takes on different connotations. It is no longer a question of a photographically captured essence, of the "punctum" that Barthes described in *Camera Lucida.* It is not a return of the particular past moment when a specific subject was in front of the camera that we are offered. Instead, we are presented with the sense of a continuous loop of images that, however, are always re-viewed according to different lights.

ANIMATION AND ANONYMITY Hope Sandrow's *They Can Only Give You Answers* (page 55) raises issues of the museum as a place of cultural ordering. The late eighteenth-century development wherein natural and cultural specimens were extrapolated from the world, reordered and displayed according to unnatural principles of classification became, a century later, an unclassifiable display as photography built its "museum without walls."

Sandrow's classifications of the past are based on visual similarities that trigger mental associations and reanimate the inanimate. Within *They Can Only Give You Answers* an ear foregrounds a van Gogh self-portrait. (In Arles, where van Gogh painted this portrait, the victorious matador would present the severed ear of his defeated bull to his lover.) A profile echoes another profile, the angled square of an Egyptian coffin is repeated in other angles above. But positions are never fixed, despite their suggested affinities. Contours are softened in the blur of movement as bodies shift (both behind and in front of the camera?) during times of exposure: Sandrow's configuration of, in her words, the "coexistence of everything at once *in flux*."[18]

The shifting figures within the photographs are ongoing portraits of people Sandrow knows. Softened by the extra instant of photographic time (a slightly prolonged moment of exposure that creates a temporal "blur"), they are renditions that are highly photographic (in the sense of a display of the medium's actual temporal chemistry) and unphotographic according to traditional expectations of recognition. As portraits, any connections to the particularity of an individual's features are blurred within the contexts of other orderings.

Passages from photograph to photograph effect disjunctions like jump cuts in a film, sudden shifts in scale and scope. The privilege of perspective is taken away; the composure of composition is upset. But the implications are those of pieces of a puzzle that can eventually be matched according to forms of (il)logic we have not yet devised.

Such implications are evident in the interlocking "T" shapes of *Measured Chaos* (page 58). It is also a "portrait," a person rendered unrecognizable through photography itself, the traditional medium of recognizable truth in portraiture. A woman becomes known by a curve of her back, echoing a curve of a hand and finger. As in all her work, Sandrow builds affinities on echoes of shapes from frame to frame, previsualizing each picture in numerous preliminary sketches.

At the same time as affinities are encouraged, joinings also are detached by Sandrow's emphasis on the photographs as separate from one another. Their seams are allowed to show their glossy buckle (to show that they are, after all, photographs). Their framings, often at different depths within the same total "piece," also make clear breaks between pictures as well as underlining the changes that occur according to a viewer's distance. From far away, an overall view explains the image. Closer, component stories emerge and disappear. Edges re-emphasize the diversity of the components, whereas the images themselves suggest singular visions. As in much postmodern photography, objects become personified and persons objectified. Rational categories of classification are dis- and re-ordered.

Robert Rauschenberg's *Photem* series (pages 57, 64) consists of overt references to the totemic in both title and structure. Central to the function of the totem is the idea of animism whereby a natural object or an animal, considered to be related to a given family or clan, is taken as its symbol. In the totemic, two principles of association are involved: similarity and contiguity, both included in the notion of "contact."[19]

Photem no. 2 puts such principles of association into visual effect. The repeated, contiguous circularity of pail, wheels, headlight, a flower, a fowl are joined within the noncausal logic of the totemic—a logic in which spatial and temporal distances do not figure, and the inanimate and animate are interchangeable according to their placements and resemblances.

Totemic structures were originally meant for obtaining mastery over man, beasts, and things, a form of magic that, as in other manifestations of magic, conflated inner and outer, private and public, into one gesture. Photography, in its beginnings, was also a form of magic and mastery, its technological modes of transference recalling more primitive modes of transference that gave the viewers and owners of its images a certain power over their subject. Rauschenberg's "photems" speak to the pull of such beliefs and to their fragile relativity.

The blocks of photographs that make up *Photem no. 17* contain propellers, an umbrella, hanging wire baskets, statuary. A sculpted head in the middle frame finds its partner in the window of a building in the frame below. Glass reflections midway suggest yet other objects that can (provisionally?) come into place. Orderings flicker at the edges of comprehension.

Baldessari's *A Healthy Life (With Jogger)* (page 35) unites its "indices" within formal structures that do not recall other structurings for the containment of beliefs such as the totem, cruciform, altar, or even (fully) a grid. His combined units do not refer to a complementary and consequential act or belief or to an "operation" of any sort. They would seem, thus, more free to return to their subjects. But, set as they are in their particular combinations, we do not necessarily understand what an indexical notation is "for." We are turned outside of the image to Baldessari's own fascination with an "incessant play of potentials." We must look "between things instead of at things," a looking paradoxical to photography.[20]

The most obvious turning out from the images themselves are the dots that cover all the faces: a primary red for the titled jogger above, white below. Both targeted and rendered anonymous, like criminals or pornographic models or simply generic cultural products, they also address the postmodern remove from the objects/subjects of photographs.

Baldessari's *Jogger* recognizes the obvious: something always is blocking our way—grid or cross or palimpsest or merely the nature of a pose. The traveler who remembers has her back to us. Media personalities are read as empty signs. Elvis's *Grace* face is never in direct address, save perhaps for one sultry lowering glance. Silvia Taccani and Christie Brinkley virtually are faceless, their features canceled by the multiplicity of their assumed personas. Novak's appropriated photograph of Ethel Rosenberg regresses into older media, losing its quality as a direct photographic trace of its subject. Blanc's cowboys and Indians are toys, Schlesinger's film actors are at a faceless remove, and so on.

In the fullness of their postmodern anonymity, Baldessari's images are jarred continually by the vertical move from one level to the next and by their disparate sizes. One experiential moment succeeds another without the organizational purposefulness imposed by various kinds of abstract orders of meaning—whether individual or social—that we associate with ordinary daily life. The pictures are, in fact, a kind of visual jogging, a funny parallel to that contemporary form of exercise which demotivates the simple activity of going somewhere (quickly) toward a variety of psychological, sociological, and medical considerations and a myriad of other possible circuities.

Baldessari's "jogged" visuality exasperates our attempts at any links, chronological or other. If Sonneman's diptychs are close to an absence of a story, Baldessari's are a plenitude of stories and absences of solutions. Such an absence of any realistic "solution," far from a return to the older noncausal narrative consciousness of primitive man (as suggested by Rauschenberg's photems) in fact, only drives us deeper into the contradictions of our own scientific causal thought modes (as do Rauschenberg's photems). Paradoxically, by cancelling a face, a story, Baldessari tells *of* it more forcefully.[21]

Are all these photographic moves and removes a matter of survival tactics in a media-glutted world? Are we seeing repeated forms of the same resistance to the erosion of meaning, activated in part by photography, of which Susan Sontag wrote in the mid-seventies?

The once radical aesthetics of juxtaposition and montage long have been assimilated by mass media and now constitute the language of corporate culture. Postmodern photography's self-conscious (sub)versions of its light contacts to persons and places, and of a juxtapositional logic, distance its imagery from its actual subjects, moving them within their normative lives. Is this only a resistance to the medium itself, which along with other media, produces, rather than represents, a world of experiences increasingly more real than the "real" world?

Photography has proved to be a most culturally susceptible medium. For a brief moment in its history, its mechanical, indexical qualities appeared to have immunized its imagery from cultural chronologies and ideologies, but, precisely because of that brief moment of belief—which still lingers—it is still vulnerable and we still are vulnerable to it.

It is certainly in part toward/against this susceptibility that the formal ploys this essay describes are directed. In part, these are resistances to the control exerted by a particularly photographic "reality" by means of which the flux of daily life is continually ordered into more elaborate, but also, in one way or another, more constraining structures.

Postmodern photographs, in their many, varied formations, discourage the kinds of fictions that are encouraged by more traditional uses of photography. We are not invited to imagine ourselves in the position of the camera. Our attention to the photographs' subjects is continually detoured. The pictures elude categorizations. Within this essay alone, numerous titles and subtitles could have been selected. Those that were chosen in no way contain the images, nor could they.

But to imply that postmodern photographic practice is merely, or even primarily, the maintenance of critical survival tactics leaves its allure unaccounted for. There is an urgency to these pictures that transcends such limitations. Their use of photography as a medium and their equally fierce denial of any traditional photographic aesthetic address more than mere exercises in protective reasoning.

In the Phillip K. Dick story, which prompted (in part) Bender's *Total Recall*, "extra-factual memory implants" can erase memories, but never desires. Postmodern attachments to photography and resistances to its conventions speak to a multitude of desires. Perhaps most central is that for a reconciliation between an inner self and an outer self that is increasingly distanced within a world that it has less and less of a role in shaping. Such a closure of meaning has never been a possibility, even in less complex times. But the desire for such resolution does not become erased or, for that matter, seized.

> Desire is always on the move: always somewhere "to the side of" the experience it presumably wants to revive, desire continually changes one image for another and is thus intrinsically an unending process of displacements and substitutions.[22]

Never a question of a Nietzschean "remembering forward" of promises to keep, nor an anticipation of a return, the al(lure) of the postmodern always is "to the side of" a closure, and a celebration of that very position.

The images refuse to depict and will not tell where they or we stand. We, as viewers, are forced back upon ourselves, upon our own labyrinths of meaning, toward the fragilities of our own delays (in glass). The images are opened prompters and carriers of our mutable assignments.

> The plotlines wander all over her
> crumbling into every digressive
> beauty . . .
>
> JORIE GRAHAM

1. Lionel Trilling, "Of This Time, Of That Place," in *The Best Short Stories of the Modern Age*, ed. Douglas Angus (Greenwich, Conn.: Fawcett, 1962). The story was first copyrighted in 1943.

2. Pamela Zoline, *The Heat Death of the Universe* (Kingston, New York: McPherson & Co., 1987), p. 14.

3. Walter Benjamin's famous phrase is from his "Short History of Photography," trans. Phil Patton, *Artforum*, Feb. 1977, p. 47.

4. Jonathan Crary, "Gretchen Bender: *Total Recall*," brochure published in conjunction with the exhibition of the same name organized by the Contemporary Arts Museum and the Museum of Fine Arts, Houston, Texas, February 1988.

5. Ibid.

6. Gérard de Nerval refers to the *gardc vuc* in "Notcs dc Voyage," *Nerval Oeuvres*, Vol. II, eds. Béguin et Richer (Paris: Pléiade, 1978). The "Notes" were first published in 1846. I am indebted to Mary Harper for this reference.

7. Nancy Goldring, "Recurrences," *Dreamworks*, vol. 4, no. 4, p. 244.

8. Donna Haraway, "Panel Discussion 3," *Inscriptions*, nos. 3/4 1988, p. 146.

9. For kinesthetic cognition specifically in relation to photography see "The Photo Ostensive (Propositions of the Phenomenal and the Mundane)" by Gerard Roger Denson, a brochure that accompanied the exhibit of the same name at the Jayne H. Baum Gallery, Spring 1988.

10. Pasadena Art Museum, 1968.

11. Artists' statement, n.d.

12. See Umberto Eco, "Innovation and Repetition: Between Modern and Post-Modern Aesthetics," *Daedalus*, vol. 114, no. 4, Fall 1985, pp. 161-183.

13. The structure has yet to be built to its full size. A maquette is shown here. The photographs are of an unnamed advertising model; Adams has used images of Donald Trump and Ronald Reagan in past installations.

14. Howard Halle, "An Interview with Dennis Adams," *Dennis Adams: Building Against the Image 1979-1987*, New York, Alternative Museum, 1987, p. 13.

15. As quoted by Eleanor Heartney, "Dennis Adams," *ARTnews*, Oct. 1986, p. 72.

16. Howard Halle, *op cit.*, p. 13.

17. Judith Williamson, *Decoding Advertisements: Ideology and Meaning in Advertising*, (London: Marion Boyard Publishers, 1978), pp. 13-14.

18. Artist's statement in *European Photography* 27, July/Aug./Sept. 1986, p. 24. Italics are mine.

19. See Sigmund Freud, *Totem and Taboo*, trans. James Strachey (New York: W.W. Norton, 1950), p. 85.

20. As quoted by Marcia Tucker, "John Baldessari: Pursuing the Unpredictable," in *John Baldessari: Work 1966–1980* (New York: The New Museum, 1981), pp. 12, 21.

21. See Fredric R. Jameson, "Beyond the Cave: Modernism and Modes of Production," in *The Horizon of Literature*, ed. Paul Hernadi (Lincoln: University of Nebraska Press, 1982), pp. 157–182.

22. Leo Bersani and Ulysse Dutoit, *The Forms of Violence: Narrative in Assyrian Art and Modern Culture* (New York: Schocken Books, 1985), p. 66.

COLLAPSE/ EXPANSION

PARALLEL REALITIES OF THE TELEVISUAL

Lori Zippay

Located at the intersection of art, technology, mass media, and the everyday, both television (the industry) and video (the medium) have engendered sophisticated electronic image-languages that reject linear narrativity and conventional pictorial logic in favor of new representational systems. Within the manipulated time and space of televisual fictions, these new electronic languages celebrate the simulated conjoinment of the real and the illusory, of parallel and simultaneous realities. Indeed, the televisual media have played a pivotal, though largely underestimated role in generating and articulating the radical, paradigmatic shifts that characterize what is understood in the late 1980s as the postmodern discourse of signification in contemporary visual art.

Subjected to rigorous social analysis as a primary determinant for the American cultural order, television also must be recognized now as a major representational determinant for much of the postmodern aesthetic order. Contained and framed within the window of the two-dimensional screen, the everyday spectacles of television routinely explode the representational logic of Renaissance perspective and classical narrative: images fracture, open up, and proliferate from within; flat space is rendered multidimensional; narratives are punctured; time is slowed or accelerated; an electronic *horra vacuii* prevails. The fragmented, surreal flow of broadcast television, with its hysterical collage of audio, visual, and informational non sequiturs (advertisements, graphics, laugh tracks, instant replays) is the most culturally diffuse articulation of the temporal, spatial, and narrative disunity that defines the strategies of much postmodern artistic practice.

The aggressively disjointed structure and fetishized consumer images of television are obvious referents for many of the media-aware texts of postmodern art (e.g. John Maggiotto, Gretchen Bender), as is the shifting position of the television viewer as receiver/consumer. Television brings the ruptured image and disrupted narrative into the home; the VCR encourages the viewer to do further violence to any sense of linearity or temporal logic on the screen. Armed with remote control, the television viewer can access brilliantly absurdist juxtapositions through random channel-zapping, further splintering through context the already fragmented television content. And the ubiquitous VCR allows the living-room savant to casually disrupt the linear flow of movies or tapes through time-shifting—propelling images and narratives forward and backward, accelerating and slowing their progress, freezing frames without leaving the couch.

By the late 1970s, modes of articulating and reading time, space, and narrative content specific to the televisual media had been translated in contemporary art into new systems of representation. By privileging aesthetic strategies such as fragmentation, pastiche, appropriation, simulation, and rupture, these televisually oriented systems subverted modernist codes of image making and narrativity and posited a media-aware order of visual signification.

In the visual arts, this postmodern "crisis of narrativity"[1] and crisis of representation have been articulated with particular resonance in specific pictorial and non-narrative strategies of contemporary film, photography, and—perhaps most dramatically—video. Although these strategies are evident in recent film and photography, it is video—the artistic medium with an incestuous relationship to the technology of broadcast television—that most clearly can achieve a meta-articulation of the televisual.

Although the media critiques of video makers are most apparent in works that appropriate and recontextualize off-air TV footage (British "scratch" video, for example),[2] a more complex media-reflexivity is engendered as artists develop idiosyncratic electronic languages that simultaneously critique and absorb the pictorial codes of television: multiple or composite imagery, disjointed narratives, the simultaneous representation of disparate temporal and spatial elements. Such structural devices, familiar as television grammar, have served as metaphorical vehicles for content in the video works of such artists as Jean-Luc Godard, Nam June Paik, Dara Birnbaum, Marcel Odenbach, and Klaus vom Bruch,[3] among others.

As with most artists working with video, these artists sustain a unique position of mutual exchange and critique in relation to the tactics and technologies that constitute television's essentially consumerist visual effects and content. While never relinquishing their critical positioning vis-a-vis the dominant mass media, they have exploited video technologies to define televisual vocabularies that enunciate and describe personal, symbolic representational systems—an alternative semiotics of the televisual. Using specific formal devices such as the multiple fracturing of the image plane, proliferation of frames within frames, image transformations, and shifting temporality—characteristic of television's arsenal of special effects—and technological postproduction devices, including the ADO, Paintbox, and Harry digital computer, video artists have inscribed television's syntax with new and idiosyncratic meaning. Their visual languages include pictorial inventions that may denote memory, suggest psychological and analogical associations, or represent a parallel past/present/future. Within these new televisual fictions, artists fuse technology and aesthetics to reference internal and external transformations and express simultaneous, parallel realities within one time and space through video.

The development of metaphorical image-languages in video has, of course, a complex, twenty-year history that encompasses the evolution of video technology and artistic practices, from early experiments with feedback to the highly evolved pictorial systems of contemporary video works. Throughout their extensive, eclectic bodies of work in video, seminal figures such as Woody and Steina Vasulka, Bill Viola, Juan Downey, and Gary Hill have constructed idiosyncratic technological vocabularies to articulate their specific theoretical and conceptual agendas.

For example, Woody Vasulka, whose development of digital image processing devices in the 1970s was instrumental in the historical evolution of video's technological grammar, has focused his later works on new modes of articulating televisual narrativity. Applying his technical inventions to his 1983 electronic opera *The Commission*, he propels his dense, fictional narrative through the proliferation, layering, and fracturing of images from within the space of the video text.

Within this context one also must cite the works of Gary Hill, in which the investigation of parallel realities—sounds/images, backwards/forwards, visual language/verbal language—has resulted in ingenious technical inventions that are precise correlatives to his conceptual base. In *Ura Aru (a backside exists)* (1985–86, 28 min.), Hill creates metatexts from visual and linguistic palindromes, applying a technological device in which written text can be sculpturally manipulated in three-dimensional space. Moving the text through a matrix of corresponding visual images and spoken words, Hill renders language concrete, uncovering and visualizing the "backside" of meaning with his metaphorical video effects.

A further illustration of the kind of idiosyncratic, televisual image-language under consideration here can be found in the later works of Dara Birnbaum. In her tapes since 1980, Birnbaum has developed an intricate video vocabulary that specifically exploits the metaphoric potential and poetic transformations of the new technologies. In the three videotapes that constitute the series *The Damnation of Faust*, Birnbaum invents new applications for sophisticated imaging devices, constructing elegant formal configurations that extend the analogical potential of her suggestive narrative content. Thematically drawn from Berlioz's *The Damnation of Faust* and formally inspired by Japanese ukiyo-e prints, Birnbaum's *Faust* series positions a woman within internal and external worlds of personal and collective memory and history. Within Birnbaum's evocative landscapes of representation, actual and psychological reality, past and present are depicted and perceived on the screen as parallel realities in a single moment of experience. To metaphorically visualize a psychological space that conjoins both external and internal realities, Birnbaum has constructed a consistent pictorial system that articulates the logic of her fictional world: frames are layered within frames; images are layered within images; dramatic wipes are construed to reveal and conceal; box inserts become windows that look onto or into those other realities.

For example, in *Will O' The Wisp* (1985, 5:40 min., color), a woman gazes from her window while the object of her gaze—children on the street below her—appear simultaneously in a small video "window" inserted within the space of her larger image. The children, themselves, can be read ambiguously as representing actual beings or objects of memory, in past or present time, an internal or external reality. Birnbaum's comments on the function of this device can be applied to much of televisual fiction: "Throughout the series there is a questioning of inner psychological space as a projected space within the space of reality, their conjoinment. There is a conjoining of the one who looks and the one who is looked at. Both are shown to us, and where does that place the viewer?"[4] Inspired by the technical sophistication of television graphics (particularly the instant replays, simultaneous inserts, and composite "live" images of network sports), Birnbaum consistently opens, divides, or otherwise expands the picture plane to inscribe the resulting parallel realities with highly evocative content.

It is more than sixty years since Walter Benjamin first charted the problematics of the technological, reproducible arts, which are historically linked to the mass media apparatus, advertising, information industries, and popular culture.[5] Although Benjamin addressed specifically the mechanical arts of printmaking, film, and photography—which certainly have a direct relation to advertising and consumer image making—even his uncannily prophetic analysis could not anticipate the dramatic revolution of the image that was occasioned by the advent of the electronic media. Here, the modernist high art/mass culture polarity achieves a delirious postmodern collapse: artists subvert and decontextualize television codes and reformulate them as pictorial inventions in service of content. These, in turn, are subverted and decontextualized by television and reformulated in commercials, sports coverage, news and entertainment graphics, and music videos.

Duality is an inherent condition of Benjamin's reproducible arts and their electronic descendants, which maintain a perverse balance between artifice and realism, between the illusory image and documentary truth. This paradoxical tension between the Image and the Real is perhaps nowhere more operative than in the time-based medium of video. On one hand, video has a strong tradition of documentary realism; when used to document or record unmediated events, video usually is perceived as more immediate, live, and "real" than film. This presumed, privileged relation to realism is evident in the standard use of video for news reportage, surveillance, the diaristic confessional. On the other hand, video also holds the unique potential for absolute artifice. Computer video technologies can generate completely artificial, synthetic electronic imagery that is highly "realistic," without having an original, real, or recorded referent. Although photographic and film images can, of course, be manipulated or altered technically, the photographic and cinematic process generally requires an actual source, a referent whose image is captured as an impression in light on emulsion.

Video, however, requires no original referent—does not even require a camera—to produce its simulated realities. Video's paradoxical embrace of both recorded realism and synthetic artifice is at the root of its radical potential for establishing a new order of visual signification. In video, this potential for dramatic manipulations hastens the collapse of the semiotic logic of causal, linear narrativity. Just as the assemblages of contemporary, multiple-image photography such as Lorie Novak's *Past Lives* derive much of their conceptual tension from the disjunction between technical image manipulation or pastiche and the perceived realism of the photographic process, so much of video's ontological meaning lies in the disruptive puncturing of the presumed phenomenological experience of the "real" by electronic manipulations. The inverse also is true: the artifice of the electronic image can likewise be punctured by an illusion of the real. Indeed, the inquiry into the dual nature of the video has historically figured as a significant aesthetic project for videomakers, and the conceptual key in the development of a metaphoric video language. When understood in the context of video's time-based properties, this project is rendered exponentially more complex.

Illustrating this confluence of the manipulated and the real, as well as the televisual subversion of representational time and space, is the *Cartes Postales* series of television works by French artist Robert Cahen. Here Cahen transforms and reframes the still photograph in time: a traditional, picturesque postcard view of a city is presented as a framed, static photograph on the video screen. Suddenly, Cahen "releases" the image through video, bringing it to life with movement and sound for a single, anecdotal moment before "freezing" it as a photograph again. As he punctures the photographic illusion with video, Cahen opens up the image onto another temporal reality, articulating an implied past, present, and future of the representational moment. Cahen's temporal trompe l'oeil extend the metaphoric potential of a metatime in video.

As in photography and film, the use of such formal devices or pictorial manipulations both acknowledges and disrupts historical, modernist traditions of the classical narrative or the realistic document, based on linguistic, literary, theatrical, and cinematic models of linear narrativity. Emerging in the years when minimalism and conceptual art had not yet been supplanted by the first of the "New Image" movements, video inherited an ambiguous relationship to narrative tradition. As an artistic practice, video's aesthetic tradition is, in fact, largely one of non-narrativity. Historically, video has celebrated image, time, and spatial manipulations, or phenomenological exercises that question the perceptual expectations of the viewer. Not burdened with a modernist legacy, video emerged as a fully post-modern art form. The conventions that it collapsed were those of the fetishized art object and commercial television: high art/mass culture.

Significantly, early representational strategies in video—as in the history of photography and film—were formulated not only in relation to artistic agendas, but also in direct relation to developments and limitations in video technology. To a greater degree than in photography or film, perhaps because of the accelerated obsolescence of electronic equipment, in video the evolution of the actual tools dramatically directed the development of an aesthetic. In the 1970s, while conceptual, site, and performance artists were constructing a radical aesthetic from the implied phenomenology of video's formal properties—including "real-time," intimate scale, simultaneity of recording and playback, time lapse—other artist/engineers were inventing prototypical image-processing devices that either artificially generated images or otherwise transformed recorded visual and audio material. One notes with irony that many of the special effects and graphics that form the canon of television's visual cliches were developed first by video artists as oppositional techniques. Throughout video's history, artists have provided the research and development for the television industry. Video and audio synthesizers, colorizers, switchers, image-processing devices—the rudiments of electronic postproduction—were first invented as art-making tools by artists such as Eric Siegel, Stephen Beck, Dan Sandin, and Nam June Paik/Shuya Abe. Other artists, working in residence in public television or industry "laboratories," were the first to develop specific strategies with the new electronic technologies that have become standard televisual syntax: the use of computerized (CMX) editing for unexpected effect, temporal devices such as slow motion, the ADO's spinning boxes and three-dimensional spatial manipulations, computer and digital languages. What were once seen as breathtaking visual inventions are now the routine fare of the music video clip.

Historically, the rich metaphoric potential engendered by this inherent paradox—realism/artifice—was rendered as content in many seminal video works. For example, Peter Campus's "classic" early work *Three Transitions* (1973, 5 min., color) is a series of phenomenological exercises that use basic strategies of multiple imaging to create succinct, almost philosophical metaphors for a psychology of the self. Campus's precise, performative pieces articulate transformations of the internal and external selves, employing video's inherent properties as metaphorical vehicle. In the first "transition," executed by shooting simultaneously with two cameras on either side of a seamless, Campus appears to stab "himself" in the back, climb through the rupture in his body, and emerge on the other side of his image.

In the second "transition," Campus frontally addresses the camera and wipes his face with his hand, thereby "erasing" the surface of his face—only to reveal another (chroma-keyed) image of his face underneath. Campus's early use of these basic video techniques remains one of video art's most potent visual inventions, in its exploitation of the medium's fundamental, formal properties and its technology to achieve metaphorical signification.

As with Campus, the performance-oriented, phenomenological investigations that characterized much of 1970s video often referenced the intimate, one-on-one scale of the medium,[6] and were most effectively realized with the artist-as-performer in a direct or "live" address to the camera. By 1980, however, video technologies and art-making strategies again had intersected, with the emphasis in video shifting from the artist/camera to the artist/postproduction. As an essentially reflexive medium, the structural and conceptual systems of video as art necessarily are dictated by the parameters of video as technology. The 1970s strategies of real-time, duration, and performance—propelled largely as a reaction against the manipulated time and content of television—yielded to an even more complex postmodern agenda. New computer video technologies were developed that advanced editing and postproduction to a privileged position, leading to the extremes of schizophrenic temporality, spatial displacements, and image metamorphoses that characterize much of post-1980 video and television.

Anomalous in the larger currents of 1970s video, but anticipating and directing the postmodern course of 1980s video, was Korean-born Fluxus artist Nam June Paik. With his neo-Dada approach to video and media, Paik created tapes that imbued his global-communications theories with an antic Pop sensibility. Using surreal visual wit and iconoclastic humor, Paik appropriated and then transformed the language of television-as-entertainment in a metacritique. Within the controlled chaos of his image-music-effects collages, Paik's accelerated time, visual and audio pastiche, and stream-of-consciousness editing functioned to reduplicate the disjunctive but seductively energetic randomness of television channel switching. Paik may have been among the first artists to acknowledge and exploit the tremendous impact of television's attention-getting audio and visual tactics; certainly he was one of the first to equate the television viewing experience with sensory pleasure. Among Paik's contributions to contemporary art was his articulation of a genuine postmodern process of exchange with the media: what he "borrowed" from television can only be matched by what television has "borrowed" from him.

Paik's seminal work *Global Groove* (1973, 28 min., color) reads as a virtual primer of the conceptual and formal devices that catalog his postmodern project of reinvesting the language of television in the metaphorical service of his juxtapositional content, which typically includes Pop iconography, a recurring cast of international avant-garde stars (Cage, Cunningham, Beuys, and others), and cross-cultural performances and artifacts. Throughout, Paik subjects this "narrative" content to an onslaught of disruptive conditions: multiplication of composite images within one frame; video and audio synthesis or desynchronization, temporal shifts, spatial manipulations, doubling, colorization, ironic juxtapositions and alterations, simultaneity of "live" and recorded elements, repetition, distortion, and fragmentation of the picture plane. Recognizing the inherent representational and conceptual potential in the technology of the medium, Paik established a radical syntax of video that appropriated, but then essentially derailed, the language of television. Though based on the very grammar of the ruptured television narrative flow, Paik's tapes routinely were considered too disruptive for American television.

Among the generation of artists explicitly influenced by Paik's combative Pop strategies was Dara Birnbaum, who in her media-reflexive critiques from the late 1970s used rigorous deconstructive tactics to dismantle television's codes of representation. Birnbaum's seminal early work featured popular television icons and pop songs—Wonder Woman, Kojak, General Hospital, disco—which were appropriated as off-air, found footage and subjected to repetition, reduction, and fragmentation through radical reediting. The result was a deconstruction of images, music, and text, which allowed for recontextualization and a dynamic critical analysis of the original text. As does Paik, Birnbaum flirts with the postmodern juncture of art and entertainment; her critiques of the ideological content embedded in television's structure are charged with the heightened visual and aural pleasure of rapid editing, seductive imagery, and visceral music. Indeed, Birnbaum's ludicrously spinning Wonder Woman, trapped forever in her magical moment of transformation by the artist's stuttering repeat edits, is one of the indelible and emblematic images of late 1970s art—a banal Pop icon whose meaning within the television text has been subverted aggressively by Birnbaum through a raw, incendiary manipulation of the medium itself.

Again, as with Paik, Birnbaum's early work reflects the process that typifies the shift to postproduction as the location for structuring meaning in video. This process is significant in that it parallels and, in fact, defines one of the critical roles of the postmodern artist. This is the artist-as-editor, reorganizing and reformulating found material—particularly those images in the public domain of pop culture—to either animate or neutralize their meaning. The artist-as-editor exercises an authorial hand; editing and postproduction techniques are imposed upon the original text to effect its conceptual transformation.

Whereas the critical re-editing of a television text is a deconstructive strategy that redefines the context of the media content (and is still a widely used video tactic), many post-production strategies of this decade focused instead on the construction of content. In certain cases, post-production *became* the content. After 1980, electronic post-production—the generation or manipulation of sound and imagery in the studio—superceded the edit as the vehicle for engendering meaning in video.

In 1980, the three-minute tape *Sunstone* by Ed Emshwiller introduced a new pictorial language for conceptualizing and visually articulating three-dimensional space in time through video. Emshwiller's electronic rendering of a sculptural, illusory "videospace" transformed the representational world of perspectival space by transforming the flat, two-dimensional video screen with a then-startling visual invention: an archetypal face is revealed to be one facet of an open, revolving cube, each side of which holds a simultaneously visible, moving video image. This iconic, spinning cube metaphorically simulates a three-dimensional space in time, a hyperreality. A pivotal tape in the electronic articulation of multiple parallel dimensions, *Sunstone* ushered in a new grammatical device for video and a banal new visual cliché for television. Emshwiller's emblematic cube, spinning through an illusory deep space and displaying simultaneous visual realities on its open surfaces, is a peculiarly apt and prescient metaphor for the televisual (dis)orientation of the postmodern 1980s.

In the late 1980s, many media artists have access to the same sophisticated digital computer devices as the television industry, which can produce electronic, hyperreal spectacles within the video space. Television networks, music video producers, advertising agencies, and media artists all share the tools to compose multidimensional, multiperspectival image-worlds, in which artificially generated and recorded images are conjoined, or else move within separate temporal and spatial planes. Here there is "no more subject, focal point, center or periphery . . . only 'information' . . . and simulacra of spaces."[7] As any illusion of causality or traditional pictorial logic is subject to collapse within this electronic simulation of totality, the viewer's position in relation to the sculpturally crafted time/space within the frame/window of the video screen is shifting, unfixed. In this televisual landscape of representation, extreme proliferations, layerings, and multiplications of concurrent images from *within* the screen (rather than from off-screen) become literal metaphors for an expanded simultaneity.

With the electronic articulation of expanded simultaneities, the televisual media make visible what in reality is invisible; they render temporality visible in space. As Jean-Paul Fargier writes, "Much more than space, it is time which becomes the spectacle in these processes . . . it corresponds to the need to *see time*."[8] Indeed, this visualization of time in space, the creation of parallel, simultaneous realities through an electronic, time-based medium, results in a unique "metatime" of the video space. The televisual language that describes these "meta" dimensions corresponds not simply to a need to see time, but to a need to experience past/present/future in one moment of time, to see front/back/sides in one space.

This ability to articulate a "metatime" in space as a literalization of parallel realities is unique to the televisual media. As such, this new, televisual order of representation challenges the established structures of other time-based image apparatuses, including those inscribed in classical narrative cinema. While Christian Metz and others have written on the psychological function of the classical cinematic text, where the narrative structure relies on the code of subconscious suture,[9] video represents not closure but rupture. Its "accelerations and decelerations, multiplications and elimination of effects [and] countless distortions lead to a complete breakdown of the centuries-old contract between the cinematic fiction and the spectator."[10] In the new televisual contract of video fiction's metatime and space, temporality may imply not causality but simultaneity, on-screen and off-screen may exist simultaneously, narratives seem to open up and emerge from within a layered collage, and the linguistic devices of metaphor and metonymy are subject to radical reapplication.

It is precisely these signifying functions of the televisual, situated at the intersection of technology and aesthetics, that artists have exploited in the 1980s to construct enigmatic, highly personal universes within which to contain their visual discourses. Unlike the epic scale of cinema, video (and television) privileges the intimate scale of the everyday, the individual melodramas of the quotidian. This intimacy has historically informed video;

in the 1960s and 1970s the video monitor became a mirror in which to explore the self and the body, while in the 1980s the monitor serves more as a window. However, video, unlike television, inverts the art historical function of the window, presenting not an outward view onto an external world, but a gaze inward that reveals internal worlds, locating visual correlatives in the dense layering and "opening up" of images from within.

For example, throughout his body of videotapes, German artist Marcel Odenbach has devised a consistent visual strategy with which to construct a psychological theater for an autobiographical discourse of identity, desire, memory, and history. Establishing an ambiguous relationship to images of sexuality, mass culture and German heritage, Odenbach uses the formal device of masking the video screen with horizontal or vertical bands of black, thereby dividing the picture plane into halves or thirds and allowing the viewer a partially blocked, voyeuristic slice of vision. Both violent and passive, the concealing black panels function to both frustrate vision and suggest the existence of a larger reality of images "behind" the surface. What slivers of images are visible become fetishized and eroticized through the censoring force of the black bands.

In later works, this formal configuration is expanded, as the screen is divided into parallel panels in which signifiers of personal memory and collective history are conjoined in one time and space. Past and present, real and mediated images are read together in the parallel time and space of Odenbach's composite screens. These masked and paneled compositions, which ironically open up charged relational systems even as they connote blockage and confinement, often suggest shuttered windows or doors that simultaneously reveal and conceal internal worlds.

A very different imaging strategy for constructing composite visual texts is used by German artist Klaus vom Bruch, who consistently exploits the device of repetitive editing of image and sound fragments, juxtaposing personal iconography with archival or media footage. With the barely suppressed violence of his reductive imagery and rapid editing, vom Bruch confronts the apparatus of historical representation and the artist's position within it. His work can be read as psychological portraits of the artist within his historical and cultural context: personal identity (as signified by vom

Bruch's face, usually seen "live") is imposed upon visual metaphors for collective, historical memory (signified by archival footage or media images) as they collide on one screen through rapid switching.

In *Das Alliiertenband* (1982, 10:30 min., color), as in many of his works, vom Bruch exercises the relatively simple technique of switching rapidly between two video sources, one live and the other recorded, to achieve one visual metaphor. Switching so quickly as to be perceived as a superimposition, vom Bruch merges his own face with aerial footage of bombed-out German cities during World War II. Vom Bruch visually occupies an ambiguous and slightly sinister space in his self-imposed role of both pilot and victim, manipulated and manipulator, ally and enemy, when his face is viewed simultaneously with the archival footage. Because it is unclear with whose point-of-view vom Bruch is identifying, the viewer's position also is rendered unclear and is, likewise, implicated in vom Bruch's loaded equation: the collapse of the personal and historical in one time.

Throughout these televisual fictions, the notion of collapse consistently, and paradoxically, signifies an expansion of meaning. Here again, one can turn to television as the model for this metaphorical implosion/expansion. Not only does its visual content collapse time and space, past and present, pictorial logic and narrativity, but the very presence of television itself within the home collapses the public and the private, the everyday and mass culture.

Whereas Birnbaum, Odenbach, and vom Bruch focus on the individual's position in relation to the media, Japanese artist Mako Idemitsu focuses on the inverse. Without employing special effects or processing techniques, Idemitsu ingeniously renders a metaspace of the televisual. Constructing melodramatic domestic narratives with an obliquely feminist subtext, she strategically positions television sets or video monitors within the diegetic space of the narrative. As the domestic scenes are played out, the video monitors reveal other, parallel realities, serving as a metaphorical space in which the psychological or internal realities of the characters are located. A woman interacts only with the video image of her absent son; the dominant image of a powerful mother on a video screen hovers over a young couple's conjugal scenes. Occupying an omnipresent, omniscient role within the sphere of domesticity, the television monitor in Idemitsu's work is a persistent signifier of the intimate positioning of the televisual in the quotidian life of a mediated society. Her narrative invention also suggests the exponential dynamics of metatime, space, sequential and simultaneous image strategies that are operative in multichannel video works, video installations, and video sculpture.

With few exceptions, all of the artists whose works have been discussed in the context of these televisual strategies also have worked extensively with installation or multichannel video. These forms extend dramatically the potential for building relational structures and parallel realities, through the simultaneous or sequential experience of multiple channels of video, and through the juxtaposition of the time/space of the video and the time/space of the installation context. As in single-channel tapes, here one encounters the visualization of expanded simultaneity, the interaction of multiple image-worlds, the juxtaposition of disparate temporal and spatial elements, the shifting position of the viewer, the fracturing and recomposition of the picture plane, metatime and metaspace. In multichannel video and installations, these systems of televisual representation acquire not only a metaphoric, but also a literal dimension.

Beyond multichannel and installation work, artists continue to push the aesthetic limits of video technologies, including the somewhat futuristic formats of interactive videodisc and satellite transmissions.

Interactive videodiscs harbor the structural and conceptual potential for actualizing a seemingly infinite system of parallel realities. With interactive videodisc technology, the viewer activates the creative process by touching the screen, unleashing either random or linear combinations and sequences of images and themes, proliferating layers of association. In a technically sophisticated parallel to the remote-control-wielding VCR viewer, the videodisc participant retains the means to shift time and manipulate the thematic progression of narrative. This is, perhaps, the ultimate vehicle for the fragmented narrative. Because multiple choices, combinations, and directions exist simultaneously within the videodisc, there is no one correct or master narrative.

For example, in one of the most fully realized interactive disc installations, Graham Weinbren and Roberta Friedman's *The Erl King* (1984–85), the artists have constructed an intricate visual discourse of psychoanalysis, history, and cultural myth. The viewer is left free to wander through this complex maze, leapfrogging randomly through time, conjuring loaded juxtapositions and sequential configurations, discovering recurrent motifs, and otherwise controlling the associative flow of narrativity and meaning. The interactive videodisc represents a kind of high-tech Pandora's box, in which an internal labyrinth of simultaneous narratives, dimensions, and realities awaits release by the curious viewer. Live satellite technologies, on the other hand, represent a kind of technological gigantism on a global scale, as distant spaces and different times are pulled together simultaneously by an omniscient eye in the sky.

Among the most theoretically and practically ambitious creations of parallel realities through technology are Nam June Paik's live, international satellite broadcasts, which include *Good Morning, Mr. Orwell* (1984), *Bye Bye Kipling* (1986) and *Wrap Around the World* (1988). Conceived as global video installations, these multinational satellite productions—while functioning as quirky, subversively "live" television entertainment—dramatically expand the metaphorical potential of technology. The mixture of "live" and recorded sources, the confluence of disparate spatial, contextual, and temporal components, the alteration and manipulation of composite images and sound—these now-standard televisual idioms are again applied in Paik's satellite broadcasts. However, here they are used not to articulate an internal world, but to reassemble the mediated and fractured external world. Paik's wild, simultaneous juxtapositions on one screen of composite images, performances, and events—broadcast live from distant continents and different time zones, and then technically processed and edited live by the artist—represent, perhaps, one of the culminating efforts in the evolution of a metaphoric electronic language for expressing an expanded simultaneity. It is as though Paik were switching televisions channels and "tuning in" live, around the world and through history. In Paik's utopian satellite links, East meets West, Orwell meets New York City in 1984, and television entertainment meets the global groove. Paik's parallel realities, in which far-flung times and spaces are collapsed into one universe contained by the video screen, are vivid signifiers of our experience of the televisual world. Positioned at the locus of technology, mass media, art, and the everyday, these televisual realities are like a hall of mirrors, a *mise en abyme*, both reflecting and being reflected in our experience of the "real" world.

As television and video technologies penetrate further into the everyday lives of an increasingly media-literate public, the paradoxical collapse and expansion of content, context, and meaning that characterize the texts of so much contemporary photography, video, advertising, and pop culture, can be seen as a direct translation of the metaphoric, technological languages of the televisual fiction.

1. Here, the application of this term refers to the interpretation set forth by Frederic Jameson in his introduction to Jean-François Lyotard's *The Postmodern Condition: A Report on Knowledge*, trans. by Geoff Bennington, Brian Massumi (Minneapolis: University of Minnesota Press, 1984).

2. *"Scratch" video* is a term used to describe a widespread style of streetwise, politicized British video that emerged in Thatcher's England in the early 1980s. As practiced by such artists as the Duvet Brothers and Guerrilla Tapes, scratch video is characterized by the low-tech pirating of off-air TV imagery, often of political figures and events, which are then ironically and irreverently re-edited, repeated, fragmented, and set to popular music. For a more thorough discussion of the scratch video phenomena, see Jeremy Welsh, "Scratch and the Surface: Contemporary British Video," *Afterimage*, January 1986.

3. Whereas Godard's preoccupation with television is evident throughout his film oeuvre, it is in his pivotal film *Numero Deux* that television becomes a crucial element in his representational system: multiple television screens, television monitors, and other such televisual framing devices are used to construct composite imagery that articulates "otherness" within the filmic space. With Anne-Marie Mieville, Godard has also produced a body of work for and about television, including the series *Six Fois Deux/Sur et Sous la Communication* (1976) and *France/Tour/Detour/Deux/Enfants* (1982), in which he investigates media in relation to the family, labor, the individual, the quotidian, and the social structure. Critiquing the production and consumption of media images in contemporary French culture, Godard and Mieville developed a reflexive image language with the video medium and the television format: slow motion, the extended take, on-screen text, the interview.

4. Robert Beck, "Artists' Profile: An Interview with Dara Birnbaum," *Media Arts* (Los Angeles: NAMAC, Fall 1988).

5. Walter Benjamin, "The Work of Art in the Age of Mechanical Reproduction," in *Illuminations*, trans. by Harry Zorn (New York: Schocken Books, 1969).

6. Perhaps the most well known and controversial consideration of this aspect of the video medium—including the Lacanian implications of the video monitor as mirror—remains Rosalind Krauss's essay, "Video: The Aesthetics of Narcissism," in *New Artists' Video*, ed. Gregory Battcock (New York: E.P. Dutton, 1978).

7. Jean Baudrillard, *Simulations*, trans. Paul Foss, Paul Patton, Phillip Beitchmann (New York: Semiotext(e), 1983), p. 53.

8. Jean-Paul Fargier, "The Hidden Side of the Moon," in *Het Lumineuze Beeld/The Luminous Image*, ed. Dorine Mignot (Amsterdam: The Stedelijk Museum, 1984), p. 40.

9. See, for example, Christian Metz, *The Imaginery Signifier: Psychoanalysis and the Cinema*, trans. Celia Britton, Annwyl Williams, Ben Brewster, Alfred Guzzetti (Bloomington: Indiana University Press, 1977).

10. Raymond Bellour, "Les Bords de la Fiction/The Limits of Fiction," trans. Jeanluc Svoboda, in *Video by Artists 2*, ed. Elke Town (Toronto: Art Metropole, 1986), p. 50.

CONTRIBUTORS

Linda Weintraub

DENNIS ADAMS, after receiving an M.F.A. from the Tyler School of Art in 1971, has pursued an art of social conscience and protest. His work has been exhibited in such institutionalized outposts for experimental art activity as the Alternative Museum, Hallwalls, the Storefront for Art and Architecture, Los Angeles County Museum of Art, The Kitchen, P.S. 122, and the Clocktower. His museum and gallery activity has been balanced with public work projects in West Germany, New York, Seattle, Evansville, San Diego.

MAC ADAMS was born in South Wales in 1943. He now makes his home in New York and exhibits internationally. The titles of the shows in which he has appeared reflect his involvement with narrative mixed media installations and consumer critiques: Visual Paradox, Photo Mannerism, Apparitions and Allusions, Photographs of the Unseen, Staged Photo Events. Exhibits have taken place at the John Michael Kohler Arts Center, Sheboygan, Wisconsin; Lawrence Oliver Gallery, Philadelphia; San Diego State University; Lijnbaan-center, Rotterdam; the Museum of Modern Art, New York;

and the La Jolla Museum of Contemporary Art (1988). He has received three NEA Fellowships (1980–82).

VIKKY ALEXANDER was born in Canada in 1959. New York City is now the center of her professional activity. She has had one-person exhibitions at CASH/Newhouse Gallery, New York, (1985–87); the Cleveland Center for Contemporary Art (1986); Galerie Pierre Huber, Geneva (1987); and Annina Nosei Gallery, New York. She was awarded visual artists' grants from Canada in four consecutive years: from 1982 to 1985.

JOHN BALDESSARI teaches at the California Institute of the Arts, Valencia. His work has been the subject of innumerable articles and books exploring his activities in book production, video, film, and photography. His work has been exhibited at such prestigious locations as the Museum of Modern Art, New York; Documenta 5; the Basel Museum, Switzerland; and, in 1989, a major retrospective of his work at the Los Angeles County Museum of Art. He has produced his own books including *Ingres and Other Parables* (1972), *Choosing String Beans* (1972), *Throwing Three Balls in the Air to Get a Straight Line* (1973).

JULIA BALLERINI received her Ph.D. from CUNY Graduate Center in 1987, writing a dissertation on early French photography of Egypt. She has taught at the School of Visual Arts, Pratt Institute, the New School for Social Research, Fordham University, The International Center of Photography, and the Tyler School of Art. Ballerini served as an editor of Out of London Press. Her reviews have appeared in *Art in America*, *Arts Magazine*, and elsewhere. She is at present a Gould Fellow at Princeton University.

GRETCHEN BENDER received her B.F.A. in 1972 from the University of North Carolina at Chapel Hill. Her work, which includes new media theater as well as photographs, has been exhibited widely in such far-flung locations as the Centre Pompidou, Paris; Los Angeles County Museum of Art; Moderna Museet, Stockholm; Institute for Contemporary Art, London; the Power Plant, Toronto; and The Kitchen, New York. She is presently completing a film.

JEAN-CHARLES BLANC was born in France in 1942. Although much of his career activity has been located in France, including an exhibition at the Centre Pompidou Musée National d'Art Moderne in Paris and at the Festival de l'Image in Le Mans, he has also been represented internationally. Blanc has had one-person exhibitions at P.S.1 Institute for Art and Urban Resources in New York, at the Edward Totah Gallery in London, and at the Galerie Claude Givaudan in Geneva.

DORIT CYPIS has stated that her work is devoted to "acting out the reciprocal mutations of self and environment." These mutations have been examined in her own living environment, which has shifted from Israel where she was born in 1951 to Canada to the United States. Her work is diverse, embracing installation, performance, photography, video, writing, and serving as the managing director of the Foundation for Art Resources based in Los Angeles. Her partners in collaboration reflect the expansive nature of her activities, and include choreographer Wendy Morris, vocalist Marilyn Habermasscher, architect Sarah Weiner, healer Russel Des Marais, composer Wendy Ultan, video artist Victor Prokopov, and writer Steve Busa.

NANCY GOLDRING is presently an associate professor of art at Montclair State College in New Jersey. She received a Fulbright Fellowship to study in Florence, Italy, after which she received an M.F.A. degree from New York University in 1970. Since that time her career has assumed a markedly international character with solo exhibitions at the Instituto d'Arte Dosso Dossi (1986) and the Galleria San Fedele (1986) in Italy, the Herzliya Museum of Art in Israel (1982), and group shows at the Terra International Exposition of International Architects at the Museum of Architecture, Wroclaw (1981) and International Center of Photography (1980) in Poland. In New York she has exhibited at the Monique Knowlton Gallery, Barbara Gladstone Gallery, A&M Artworks, and Jayne H. Baum Gallery.

WILLIAM LARSON studied at the Illinois Institute of Technology, taught for many years at the Tyler School of Art, and is currently Director of Graduate Studies in Photography at the Maryland Institute, Baltimore. He has been the recipient of several fellowships, including a Guggenheim in

1982. Since 1968 his work has been exhibited at such locations as the Los Angeles County Museum of Art (1987), the Muenchner Stadtmuseum (1985), Princeton University (1983), International Museum of Photography at George Eastman House (1983), the Los Angeles Institute of Contemporary Art (1978), and the Museum of Modern Art, New York (1984, 1978, 1973).

JOHN MAGGIOTTO graduated from the State University of New York at Buffalo in 1977. Since then he has had solo exhibitions at White Columns, New York, and the Los Angeles Institute of Contemporary Art, and has participated in group exhibitions such as "In Western New York" at Albright-Knox Art Gallery, Buffalo, (1979); "Hall Walls, Five Years" at the New Museum, New York (1980); "Avant-Garde in the Eighties" at Los Angeles County Museum of Art (1987); and "Poetic Injury, The Surrealist Legacy in Post-Modern Photography" at the Alternative Museum, New York (1987).

LORIE NOVAK teaches at the Tisch School of Arts, New York University and the School of Visual Arts in New York. She has integrated into an active exhibition schedule such multimedia activities as dance/slide collaborations with choreographer Victoria Marks and artist Janet Zweig. Her work is included in the collection of the Art Institute of Chicago; Bibliotheque Nationale, Paris; Harvard University's Fogg Art Museum; Museum of Fine Arts, Boston; International Center of Photography, New York; Museum of Modern Art, New York, and elsewhere.

ROBERT RAUSCHENBERG spent his formative years at the Kansas City Art Institute (1946–1947), Black Mountain College (1948–1949), and the Art Students League (1949–1950) and has earned a vast exhibition record that includes retrospective exhibitions in the LA Museum, Copenhagen; Baltimore Museum of Art; Tate Gallery, London; Pompidou Center, Paris, National Collection of Fine Art; Museum of Modern Art, New York; Whitney Museum of American Art; Albright-Knox Gallery; and elsewhere.

HOPE SANDROW was born and educated in Philadelphia. However, she has concentrated her professional activity in the East Village. Her work has been selected as a representation of experimental, contemporary photography at the Philadelphia College of Art (1989); the National Museum of American Art (1989); the Baltimore Museum of Art (1987); the Whitney Museum branches in Fairfield, Connecticut, and at the Equitable Center (1987); the Hirshhorn Museum (1986); the Cologne and the Zurich Art Fairs (1984); and at the Indianapolis Biennial (1986). In New York her work has been shown at the Gracie Mansion Gallery (1988, 1984) and in *Investigations* at the International Center of Photography (1984).

JOHN SCHLESINGER has exhibited nationally since 1983. During these years, his work has also been included in "Technics" and "Poetic Injury" at the Alternative Museum, "Wider Perspectives" at the Museum of Contemporary Photography in Chicago, "Unidentified Flying Object" at the Gracie Mansion Gallery in New York, "Recent Acquisitions" at the Museum of Modern Art. Schlesinger has been awarded two NEA Fellowships (1988, 1986), was born in 1954, and resides in Brooklyn.

KLAUS SCHNITZER has taught in the Fine Arts Department of Montclair State College since 1971. His first degrees were in social and political science including graduate work at the State University of New York in Albany. He earned an M.F.A. from Ohio University, Athens, in 1971. Since 1977 he has worked collaboratively with Robert Sennhauser. Together they received an NEA grant (1980) and have been represented in such shows as "A Breath of Light," New Jersey State Museum; "Word Image," San Antonio Art Institute; "Contemporary Photography as Fantasy," Loyola Marymount University; "The Contemporary Platinotype," Rochester Institute of Technology.

ROBERT SENNHAUSER received a B.F.A. (1972) and an M.F.A. (1974) in printmaking from Ohio University's School of Art in Athens. He is a cofounder of Artists Book Works in Chicago, as well as a performance artist. Both his "live" art and his photographs have been viewed frequently throughout the United States. He has been visiting artist at the San Antonio Art Institute (1984–85), the Chicago Art Institute (1982–84), and the University of Oklahoma (1977–78).

EVE SONNEMAN, born in Chicago, educated at the University of Illinois and the University of New Mexico, where she received her M.F.A. in 1969, has had an extensive series of one-person exhibitions. These include Leo Castelli Gallery (1986, 1984, 1982, 1980, 1978, 1976), the Tyler School of Art (1986), the Museum of Modern Art in Costa Rica (1985), Centre Georges Pompidou (1984), Santa Barbara Museum of Art (1984), the Contemporary Arts Center in New Orleans (1980). Her other activities include the publication of three books (*The American Cottage Garden*, 1989, *Roses are Read*, 1982, and *Real Time*, 1976), and teaching, (Cooper Union College of Art and Architecture, 1985 and 1975–78; School of Visual Arts, 1975–1988).

SILVIA TACCANI was born in Italy and now lives and works in Connecticut. She was educated at the Rhode Island School of Design, Brown University, and Fleming College in Italy. During the past six years her work has been presented at the Florida Institute of Technology; Real Art Ways, Hartford, Connecticut; Rizzoli Gallery, Texas; Nexus Contemporary Art Center, Atlanta, Georgia; Gallery Z in New York City; and elsewhere.

WILLIAM S. WILSON has been a member of the Department of English at Queens College since 1961. He received a B.A. from the University of Virginia, and M.A. and Ph.D. degrees from Yale University. He is best known for his book of stories entitled *Why I Don't Write Like Franz Kafka* published by Ecco Press in 1977 and 1985, and *Birthplace: Moving into Nearness*, North Point Press, 1982. He has also written reviews in the *American Book Review* and *The New York Times Book Review* and essays on art for *Antaeus*.

BRIAN WOOD had his first solo show in 1979 at the Galerie Marielle Mailhot in Montreal in 1979. Since that time he has had one-person exhibitions at such galleries as the Marcuse Pfeifer Gallery in New York and the McIntosh/Drysdale Gallery in Washington D.C., and group exhibitions at the Virginia Museum of Fine Arts; Photographers' Gallery, London; Everson Museum of Art, Syracuse; Museum of Modern Art, New York; and the Brooklyn Museum. Wood was born in Canada and received his B.A. there from the University of Saskatchewan. In 1984 he received his M.A. degree from Hunter College in New York, where he currently resides.

LORI ZIPPAY graduated from Bard College in 1980. A year later she joined the staff at the Electronic Arts Intermix as an administrative assistant after having served as assistant in the Video Department at the Museum of Modern Art. She collaborated with Barbara London in preparing the "Chronology of Video Activity in the U.S. from 1965 to 1980," which appeared in the September 1980 issue of *Artforum* and was also a contributor to the Fall 1985 issue of the *Art Bulletin* on video. She currently serves as the Director of Electronic Arts Intermix.

CHECKLIST

(Note: Unless otherwise indicated, all dimensions are in inches. Height precedes width.)

DENNIS ADAMS *Ba(bb)le: Podium for Dissent*, 1984. Maquette, 110¾ × 14¼ × 18 on a 1½- or 4-foot pedestal (scale: 2½″ = 1′). Plastic, aluminum, brass, enamel, fluorescent light, duratans. Courtesy Nature Morte gallery.

MAC ADAMS *Trapped*, 1986. 72 × 48, C Print. / *Interrogation*, 1986. 40 × 30, C Print. Courtesy Farideh Cadot gallery.

VIKKY ALEXANDER *Obsession*, 1983. 12 panels, each 36 × 24, which can be combined in different configurations. Silver prints with yellow plexi. / *Grace*, 1984. 112 × 48. Mixed media. Courtesy CASH/Newhouse gallery.

JOHN BALDESSARI *A Healthy Life (With Jogger)*, 1987. 62½ × 84¼, black-and-white photographs, acrylic. Courtesy Sonnabend gallery.

GRETCHEN BENDER Untitled from *Total Recall* series, 1986. 60 × 96, steel, fluorescent lights, TV film strips. Courtesy Nature Morte gallery.

JEAN-CHARLES BLANC *Painted Desert*, 1983–86. 11¼ × 41½ × 1, Polaroid photographs mirror, paint, gold-leaf frame. / *Last News from the West*, 1983–86. 11¼ × 41½ × 1, Polaroid photographs, mirror, paint, gold-leaf frame. Courtesy the artist.

DORIT CYPIS *Love After Death*, 1986, one of a triptych. 40 × 39, Cibachrome and C prints with acrylic frames. Courtesy the artist.

NANCY GOLDRING *The Traveler Remembers*, 1987. 39¾ × 66½, six Cibachrome prints, each 16 × 20. Courtesy Jayne H. Baum gallery.

WILLIAM LARSON *Lexigraphic Portrait: Newsweek/Harpers*, 1987. 40 × 64, black-and-white photographs. / *Lexigraphic Portrait: Moda/Grif*, 1987. 40 × 64, black-and-white photographs. Courtesy the artist.

JOHN MAGGIOTTO Untitled, 1987. 20 × 60 (three 20 × 20 panels), photographic emulsion on plaster base. / Untitled, 1988. 17 × 35, photographic emulsion on plaster base. Courtesy artist.

LORIE NOVAK *Fragments*, 1987. 26 × 36, Cibachrome print. / *Past Lives*, 1987. 36 × 29, Cibachrome print. Courtesy Lieberman & Saul gallery.

ROBERT RAUSCHENBERG *Photem Series I, no. 2*, 1981. 54¾ × 46½, black-and-white photographs. / *Photem Series I, no. 17*, 1981. 68¾ × 16, black-and-white photographs. Courtesy Leo Castelli gallery.

HOPE SANDROW *They Can Only Give You Answers*, 1986. 69 × 19, silver prints. / *Measured Chaos*, 1988. 65 × 60, silver prints. Courtesy Gracie Mansion gallery.

JOHN SCHLESINGER Untitled, 1987 60 × 40, selenium toned black-and-white prints. / Untitled, 1988. 15 × 60, selenium toned black-and-white prints. Courtesy the artist.

KLAUS SCHNITZER / ROBERT SENNHAUSER *Timerman's Dream* from *Terrorist Series*, 1986. 36 × 60, platinum prints. Courtesy the artists.

EVE SONNEMAN *Starfish, New Mexico*, 1980. 8 × 20, Cibachrome (each print is 8 × 10). / *Newspaper, N.Y.*, 1980. 8 × 20, Cibachrome (each print is 8 × 10). Courtesy Castelli Graphics.

SILVIA TACCANI *#91–1986*, 1986. 38 × 40, Polaroids. / *#97–1987*, 1987. 40 × 42, Polaroids. Courtesy the artist.

BRIAN WOOD *Sanctuaries*, 1980. 45 × 63, color and black-and-white photographs, four panels. / *Altar*, 1980. 47½ × 29, color and black-and-white photographs, two panels. Courtesy Lieberman & Saul gallery.

The staff at Aperture for *Sequence (con)Sequence*
is Michael E. Hoffman, Executive Director;
Steve Dietz, Editor; Lisa Rosset, Managing Editor;
Barbara Levine, Assistant Editor;
Stevan Baron, Vice President, Production;
Sarah Adams, Miranda Ottewell, Editorial Work-Scholars.
Book design by Wendy Byrne.

Aperture Foundation, Inc., publishes a periodical,
books, and portfolios of fine photography
to communicate with creative people everywhere.
A complete catalog is available upon request.
Address: 20 East 23 Street, New York, New York 10010.